A Church in Transition

A Devotional Commentary on 1 Timothy through Hebrews

A CHURCH IN TRANSITION

*A Devotional Commentary
on 1 Timothy through Hebrews*

GENERAL EDITOR

Leo Zanchettin

The Word Among Us Press
9639 Doctor Perry Road
Ijamsville, Maryland 21754
www.wordamongus.org

08 07 06 05 04   1 2 3 4 5 6
ISBN: 1-59325-055-X

Cover design by David Crosson

Made and printed in the United States of America.

Library of Congress Control Number: 2005924964

Table of Contents

Acknowledgments

I'd like to thank everyone who has made this commentary possible, especially all of the writers who contributed meditations. Some of the meditations appearing in this book were initially developed for *The Word Among Us* monthly publication, and I am grateful to these writers for granting us permission to reprint their work. I also want to thank Fr. Joseph Mindling, OFM Cap, Fr. Joseph Wimmer, OSA, Fr. George Montague, SM, and Fr. Jude Winkler, OFM Conv, for contributing the introductory chapters. A special note of thanks also goes to Bob French, Jill Boughton, Hallie Riedel, and Jeanne Kun for their considerable contributions to the meditations. And finally, I want to thank Margaret Procario for her clear-headed (and good-humored!) editing of the manuscript, and Kathy Mayne, for her tireless administrative work in gathering all the material that went into this book. Thanks, too, to Patricia Mitchell, editor of The Word Among Us Press, without whose deadline flexibility and words of encouragement this book would not have been completed. May the Lord abundantly bless each of them!

Leo Zanchettin

Introduction
"Remember Jesus Christ . . ."
Godly Wisdom for Times of Change and Transition

by Leo Zanchettin

A young married couple buys their first house. . . .

A man in his forties decides to switch careers in midstream. . . .

A thirty-five-year-old woman stands at the coffin of her mother, who has died unexpectedly. . . .

A young seminarian lies prostrate before his bishop, about to be ordained a priest. . . .

A pregnant woman feels her baby stirring and ponders the new life within her. . . .

No matter who we are, we can all remember specific moments like these, when our lives took a dramatic turn or we had to adjust to a new reality. Some of those changes may have triggered feelings of anxiety and worry, while others may have generated a sense of excitement and eager anticipation. But no matter how we reacted, we recognized that we were turning a corner and could never go back to the way things had been before.

Thinking back to times of change and transition in our lives can give us a good perspective as we ponder the letters contained in this devotional commentary. Each in its own way reflects the early church at a time of transition from a loosely organized collection of converts clinging to outmoded laws and social structures to an established church community under the direction of a new generation of leaders and ready to embrace all the implications of a new life in Christ. And in each letter, we find Spirit-filled words of wisdom, comfort, and challenge aimed at helping believers embrace these changes peacefully and confidently.

Navigating the Waters of Change. In 1 and 2 Timothy and Titus, we see small house churches dealing with the loss of their mentor, Paul, and adapting to a new generation of leaders who had no contact with the original apostles. Would these new leaders be as charismatic? As wise? As motivating?

And would the intimacy and uniqueness that had characterized these small churches survive as they joined with other congregations? Or would they all dissolve into one homogeneous mass?

The Letter to Philemon presents a wealthy young man faced with the challenge of forgiving his runaway slave Onesimus and welcoming him back as a brother in Christ. As a convert to Christianity himself, Philemon had enjoyed the freedom and love of his newfound life in Christ. But now he had to decide whether to allow that conversion to rearrange not only the way he ran his household, but the very class structure by which he had lived. Philemon may already have sensed that the social order he had taken for granted was beginning to weaken; in responding to this new challenge, he had to decide whether to fully embrace the brotherly love of Christianity or cling to his former way of life.

In the Letter to the Hebrews, we find believers who have to distance themselves from the comfortable familiarity of their Jewish upbringing so that they can accept the new covenant that Jesus initiated. Just as their Hebrew ancestors had to learn a new way of living during their desert journey out of Egypt, so too these Hebrew Christians, who were on their way to a new promised land in Christ, had to put aside the old religious structures that had given them such assurance. The sacrifices of the temple could not support their new life in Christ, and they had to learn to live by a deeper kind of faith and a more intimate way of worship. A new and living way into God's presence had opened up for them. But they could not enter through it with all the baggage of the past—which proved more difficult to discard than they ever expected.

"Remember Jesus Christ . . ." Part of the challenge in any transition we face is knowing what to keep from the old as we embrace the new. The churches of 1 and 2 Timothy and Titus needed to maintain the sense of intimacy and community that the believers had experienced in their small house-church environments even as they welcomed new members and made room for a new generation. Philemon had to receive Onesimus back as a brother and yet retain a sense of harmony and balance in his household. The Jewish Christians addressed in Hebrews needed to step into the freedom from the law that Jesus had won, all the while holding on to the heart and soul of God's revelation to Moses and the prophets.

And what about us? Each of the transitions we must make in our own lives will present us with a unique set of challenges. Will we be able to accept the aspects of our lives that have changed and make our best effort to grow and thrive in our new way of life? Or will we refuse to change, blindly clinging to the remnants of our former lifestyle?

The only sure way to navigate the waters of change is to follow the advice offered in each of the letters in this book. In different ways, every one of them presents the same wisdom: When faced with upheavals in your life, don't let the turmoil unsettle you. Anchor yourself in your faith, and let that faith steady you through the turbulence. With Christ as your rudder, go back to the truths of the gospel, and let them guide you on your course: "Remember Jesus Christ, raised from the dead" (2 Timothy 2:8). "I pray that the sharing of your faith may become effective" (Philemon 6). "We must pay greater attention to what we have heard, so that we do not drift away from it" (Hebrews 2:1).

Every time we return to the heart of the gospel, to Jesus Christ and his saving, intimate love for us, we will find the rest, the strength, the confidence, and the direction that we need. We will embrace every transition with hope, knowing that we have inherited a kingdom that can never be shaken, no matter how powerful the currents of change (Hebrews 12:28).

May the meditations in this commentary help us all to put our lives and our hope in Christ, who will guide us with his love to treasure our pasts, embrace our presents, and look forward to our futures in him—despite any transitions life may bring our way.

"In Memory of Me . . ."
Early Christian Eucharistic Celebrations

by Fr. Joseph F. Wimmer, OSA

There is something rather predictable for us twenty-first-century believers when we go to Mass. We know when we will sit, stand, or kneel. We know that we will hear the word of God proclaimed before the bread and wine are transformed into Jesus' body and blood. We know that after Communion, we will have a brief time for silent prayer and meditation, perhaps accompanied by some music. Of course, there is the unpredictable side, such as not knowing what the homily will consist of, and even better, not knowing exactly how God will touch us as we worship him and receive his Son. But at least as far as form and structure are concerned, the Mass is rather well established.

Now, try to contrast this predictability with the experience of the first generation of believers. Nothing had been formalized. There were no official eucharistic prayers yet. No missalettes told the worshippers when to kneel, or even which passages from the Hebrew Scriptures were to be read each Sunday. And the gospels hadn't even been written yet! Even in this most familiar of celebrations—the Eucharist—the first-century church was a church in transition, moving from a series of loose congregations to the beginnings of a structured institution with recognized leadership and a body of doctrine. Let's take a look at some of the differences in the way that the church's first and second generations celebrated the Eucharist.

Transforming an Ancient Feast. At the Last Supper, on the night before he was crucified, Jesus told his disciples, "This is my body. This is my blood. Do this in memory of me." With these few words, he transformed the ancient Jewish Passover feast into a celebration of the new covenant and a new relationship with the Father.

After Jesus rose and ascended into heaven, the apostles and first Christians gathered for the meal as Jesus had told them to. Repeating Jesus' words, "This is my body; this is my blood," they became aware of his presence among them. Jesus had not abandoned them! Though seated in heaven, he still remained close—invisible but *there*, in a mysterious but real way as their Lord and brother.

The early Christians knew that this gift was not just for their own enjoyment. It was to be shared with others in the "breaking of the bread," in the unity of their love of God and love of neighbor. According to John, even the Last Supper began with an extraordinary lesson of humble service: Jesus washed his disciples' feet and told them, "I have set you an example, that you also should do as I have done to you" (John 13:15).

The Earliest Traditions. Although the Christian celebration of Jesus' gift of himself was sometimes called the Lord's supper (1 Corinthians 11:20), it was more commonly referred to in these early days as the "breaking of the bread." Why? Meals in ancient Jewish homes always began with a blessing of bread by the head of the household, who would then break it with his hands and give a piece to every person at the table. It was a way of thanking God for the food and uniting the members around the table. The Last Supper would have begun the same way, and the first Christians simply referred to it by this initial rite, the "breaking of the bread." It wasn't until early in the second century that it came to be known as the "Eucharist," a Greek word meaning "thanksgiving."

It's not clear how frequently the early Christians celebrated this special meal, but they probably did so at least once a week. In Semitic culture the day began at sunset, so Sunday, or the "first day of the week" (Acts 20:7; 1 Corinthians 16:2), actually began on Saturday evening. In describing the life of the early Christians, Luke says that they "devoted themselves to the apostles' teaching and fellowship, to the breaking of bread and the prayers" (Acts 2:42). By listing the breaking of the bread with apostolic teaching and prayer, Luke shows that the meal was special. And by including fellowship in the list, he adds the important dimension of believers sharing their lives with one another.

A few verses later Luke again remarks, "Day by day, as they spent much time together in the temple, they broke bread at home and ate their food with glad and generous hearts" (Acts 2:46). Once more he mentions a frequent ritual ("day by day") involving a meal in someone's home and an openness to sharing it generously with others.

We get still another glimpse of an early Communion celebration later in the Acts of the Apostles. Luke explains that he and Paul had stayed a week at Troas in Asia Minor and that Paul was about to depart. He writes:

> On the first day of the week, when we met to break bread, Paul was holding a discussion with them; since he intended to leave the next day, he continued speaking until midnight. There were many lamps in the room upstairs where we were meeting. A young man named Eutychus, who was sitting in the window, began to sink off into a deep sleep while Paul talked still longer. Overcome by sleep, he fell to the ground three floors below and was picked up dead. But Paul went down, and bending over him took him in his arms, and said,

> "Do not be alarmed, for his life is in him." Then Paul went upstairs, and after he had broken bread and eaten, he continued to converse with them until dawn; then he left. Meanwhile they had taken the boy away alive and were not a little comforted. (Acts 20:7-12)

Apparently Paul presided over the "breaking of the bread," which began in the evening and included a very long talk. Luke shows that it was a liturgy and not just a plain meal when he speaks about the lighting of "many lamps." Even the story of Eutychus reveals an essential aspect of this celebration: Union with one another around the table of the Lord necessarily included concern for the physical well-being of one another.

Eucharist in the Morning. By the first half of the second century A.D., Christian eucharistic services were held on Sunday morning and were no longer part of communal meals. Perhaps the crowds were simply getting too large, or perhaps abuses had crept back into community dinners. At times the people prayed throughout the night and ended their vigil with a eucharistic celebration in the morning. Our knowledge of these practices is limited, but we do have a text from about A.D. 150, St. Justin's *First Apology*, which describes a Christian eucharistic celebration on Sunday morning with a liturgy modeled on the Jewish synagogue service. He writes:

> We greet one another with a kiss. Then bread and a cup containing wine mixed with water are brought to the one who presides over the brethren; he takes them and offers prayers, glorifying the Father of all things through the name of the Son and the Holy Spirit. . . . When the prayer of thanksgiving is ended, all the people present give their assent with an "Amen!" . . . Deacons distribute the bread and the wine and water. . . . This food we call "Eucharist," . . . for we do

not receive these things as though they were ordinary food and drink. . . . for the food over which the thanksgiving has been spoken becomes the flesh and blood of the incarnate Jesus, in order to nourish and transform our flesh and blood. (Chapters 65–67)

Justin also includes the words of consecration and notes that the "memoirs of the apostles or the writings of the prophets" were read and proclaimed by the presider, "admonishing and exhorting us to imitate the splendid things we have heard." An offertory collection was taken up for those in need: widows, orphans, the sick, visiting strangers, and others. They even prayed the Our Father together. In so many ways, this description mirrors the structure of the Mass as it still exists today.

Prayers and Exhortations from the Fathers. The earliest complete text of a eucharistic liturgy that we have was recorded by St. Hippolytus of Rome around A.D. 215. Modeled on Jewish prayers after meals, it includes the words of consecration and a remembrance of Jesus' redemptive work. Now, with the liturgical reforms of Vatican II, this ancient prayer has been reclaimed and is in use today as Eucharistic Prayer II.

In addition to specific prayers, Jesus' gift of the Eucharist inspired many early Christian writers to express their joyous praise and thanks, and to remind believers of the need for unity and charity.

St. Ignatius, bishop of Antioch, was arrested by the Roman authorities about A.D. 107 and sentenced to be thrown to wild beasts for his faith. On his way to Rome he wrote seven letters, some of which included descriptions of the Eucharist: "Be careful then to participate in only the one Eucharist, for there is only one flesh of our Lord Jesus and one cup to unite us in his blood, one altar, just as there is one bishop"

(*Philadelphians*, 4). "My desire is for the bread of God, which is the flesh of Jesus Christ, and for drink I desire his blood, which is incorruptible love" (*Ephesians*, 7, 2-3). In these letters Ignatius reminds the people of the two-fold commandment of love and adds, "Those who profess themselves to be Christ's are known not only by what they say, but by what they practice" (*Ephesians*, 14).

St. Leo the Great, the bishop of Rome who faced down Attila the Hun in A.D. 452, gave many sermons on caring for those in need. He also emphasized the reality of Jesus' eucharistic presence and our intimate union with him:

> Even the tongues of infants do not keep silence upon the truth of Christ's body and blood at the rite of Holy Communion. For in that mystic distribution of spiritual nourishment, what is given and taken is of such a kind that in receiving the power of the heavenly food we pass into the flesh of him who became our flesh. (*Letter*, 59)

An Unchanging Promise. While it took centuries for the Mass to become as developed as it is today, the convictions of the early Christians—as well as the miracle of transubstantiation that they experienced—haven't changed a bit. From across the centuries, these first believers in Christ continue to call us to receive Jesus into our hearts with humble joy and gratitude, even as they call us to open our hearts in generous love for those around us. Jesus Christ is the same yesterday, today, and forever (Hebrews 13:8). No matter what form our worship of him takes, he continues to be present in so many ways: gloriously at the right hand of the Father, on the altar at Mass, in our hearts, and even in the "distressing disguise of the poorest of the poor" (Mother Teresa).

A Vital Letter at a Critical Moment

The First Letter to Timothy

A Vital Letter at a Critical Moment

A Vital Letter at a Critical Moment
An Introduction to the First Letter to Timothy

by Fr. Jude Winkler, OFM Conv

There comes a time in the life of any new movement when it must address the need to institutionalize. While the enthusiasm and vision of its founders are vital for the group to come together, they are not the only necessary ingredients to ensure its survival in the long run. For that, it needs structure, guidelines, and stability. This is especially the case when differing opinions of the group's purpose threaten to divide it before it becomes well established.

The First Letter to Timothy marks just such a moment in the life of the early church. It came at a time when Christianity ceased to be a loose amalgam of enthusiastic believers and became a church: an organization with a structure, a set of guidelines for its members, and an identity all its own. There are references to a hierarchy of leaders—at least some of whom were paid—and the letter speaks of professions of faith that all its members were expected to accept. This was not a letter addressed to a newly founded church. The Ephesus described here was an actual, ecclesial community with a life all its own.

Who Wrote It and When. The letter purports to have been written by St. Paul to his disciple Timothy, who was the leader of the church in Ephesus. Today, however, many scholars doubt that Paul actually wrote it. The structure of the church and the specific way its beliefs are spelled out seem to date to a period a couple of decades after Paul's execution in Rome. Even the vocabulary and manner of writing found in this letter appear to be significantly different from the writing style that Paul used in letters like 1 Corinthians, Romans, and Philippians.

While it seems odd to us that someone would write a letter and then attribute it to another person, this was a common practice in the ancient world. If Paul did not actually write the letter, then its author—probably a loyal disciple of Paul's who wanted to adapt the apostle's teaching to the situation at Ephesus—wrote in his name so that it would share in his authority.

Ultimately, it doesn't make a lot of difference to us who actually wrote 1 Timothy. Whoever the original human author was, the church has always considered it to be inspired by the Holy Spirit and has consistently looked to it as an important witness to a critical moment in Christian history.

Timothy and Ephesus. So who is the Timothy to whom this letter was addressed? He was one of Paul's first disciples and a co-worker with him in the work of evangelizing and establishing churches. Timothy's mother, Eunice, was Jewish, while his father was pagan. The fact that Timothy had not been circumcised by the time he was a young man leads us to believe that he grew up in a home where his Father's beliefs held sway—despite his mother's deep faith and love for the Hebrew Scriptures (Acts 16:1-3; 2 Timothy 1:5; 3:15).

Tradition holds that Timothy was the first bishop of the church at Ephesus. Paul had preached in Ephesus—one of the great cities of the Roman Empire—for two years, and he held the members of the community in deep affection (Acts 20:17-38). From information contained in the Bible and other documents from the time, we also know that the church in Ephesus suffered from a serious outbreak of heresy.

It's not surprising, then, that 1 Timothy mentions heresy several times. We read that there were some in the church who busied themselves with endless myths and genealogies (1 Timothy 1:4). They called themselves "teachers of the law" and practiced a rigorous form of asceticism, even forbidding marriage (1:7; 4:1-3). They rejected the goodness of creation (4:4). They also sought their own personal gain and not that of the community (6:3-5).

Given all of these details, we can safely say that the people teaching these things were following the tenets of an early form of Gnosticism. The Greek word *gnosis* means "knowledge," and these people claimed to have a special, spiritual revelation that was superior to the revelation of the gospel—a revelation that made them superior to other Christians, as well. Rejecting the material world as sinful and corrupt, they went to one of two extremes: Either they practiced an exaggerated form of asceticism and self-denial, or considering themselves above corruption, they threw themselves into all kinds of licentiousness, holding that "to the pure all things are pure" (see Titus 1:15). Interestingly, both extremes are evident in this letter.

Virtue Lies in the Middle. As is almost always the case, the truth lies not in either of the two extremes of Gnosticism but somewhere in between them. God created the world as good, and Christians are not meant to reject it or consider it evil. Scripture teaches that we can experience God's goodness and kindness in creation through such blessings as food, marriage, and even the beauty of nature. Yet because of sin, it is easy for us to misuse and abuse these good things, so we have to be careful how we approach the world. This is the purpose of a balanced and not exaggerated form of asceticism (1 Timothy 4:7-10; 6:7-10).

We fast from food not because it is evil but rather so that we can learn how to use it properly. Sex is good, but it is intended to be used as a way for a married couple to share their love with each other. Beautiful things can bring us closer to God, or they can lead us astray by becoming too important to us, as possessions can begin to possess us. As St. Augustine says, extremes are not good, and virtue lies in the middle.

1 Timothy addresses this balance when it presents a long series of teachings concerning the proper way for Christians to act. There are instructions concerning the character and qualifications of bishops (*episcopos*), deacons, elders (*presbyteros*), men, women, widows, families, and even slaves. Far from being a simple catalog of virtues, this letter makes it clear that no matter what our state in life, it is possible for us to live a life of exemplary virtue.

Early Church Structure. We sometimes forget that the hierarchy of the first-century church developed gradually as the Spirit guided the church to respond to the needs of the community. In this letter, we see three titles that sound strikingly familiar to us: bishop, deacon, and presbyter. The words may sound the same, but we cannot be sure whether the responsibilities of each of these positions correspond completely to what they entail today. Let's take a look at each of them to see what they may have meant for the first-century church.

We first hear about the *episcopos*, a word that literally means "overseer" and that we translate as "bishop." Bishops in the early church were married, and the bishop's guidance of his own family was, in fact, an indication of how he would run the church. As the leader of the church in a particular area, the bishop was to be sober, modest, peaceful, and able to get along with people.

There were also deacons (*diakonous* in Greek). As assistants to the bishop, they too were to be sober and not greedy and were expected to be faithful teachers as well as good family men. 1 Timothy 3:11 adds that "women likewise must be serious, not slanderers, but temperate, faithful in all things." There are two possible ways to translate and interpret this line, because the same word in Greek can be translated as either "women" or "wives." So is the author referring to the women who are deacons or to the women who are deacons' wives? We do know that there were female deacons in the early church, and chances are that this line is a reference to them, even if we don't know exactly what they did. For if the author had intended to write about the deacons' wives, he probably would have said "*their* women."

Later in the letter we hear about the presbyters, who are also called the elders. We normally interpret this term as a reference to priests, but its meaning isn't entirely clear here. Since no list of requirements is spelled out for the office of presbyter, it is possible that the author is using this phrase as a generic term to refer to the bishops and deacons who together would make up the ruling elders of the church.

In addition to the hierarchy mentioned above, 1 Timothy deals with a church institution that no longer exists: the order of widows (1 Timothy 5:9-16). We don't have much information about this association. All we do know is that the church cared for its members who were in need by providing for widows who were more than sixty years old and had no family of their own. This "order of widows" gives us a good example of how a misfortune can become an opportunity. Widows were encouraged not to become ensnared by loneliness and self-pity but to use their time and resources for the good of others. Of course life can be painful at times and can leave us off balance and even depressed. But if we retreat into ourselves for too long, we only prolong our misery. If, on the other hand, we force ourselves to reach out beyond ourselves, we will gradually find peace and even fulfillment.

Praying for Peace. The people of Paul's and Timothy's time were subject to a series of dishonest rulers, and Christians, in particular, were frequently objects of persecution. So it's not surprising that 1 Timothy would advocate prayer not only as a means of spreading the gospel but also as a way of promoting peace.

To encourage rulers to govern justly, the people are urged to offer supplications, prayers, intercessions, and thanksgivings for them. That is the right thing to do, even if the rulers are corrupt, because God wants everyone to know the truth and Christ's sacrifice has won salvation for all (1 Timothy 2:4). Praying for peace would also make the people behave civilly toward each other, for men are instructed to lift "holy" hands to God without resorting to anger or argument (2:8).

Advice for Women, Families, and Households. While men are exhorted to pray, women are to conform to the norms of the day—remaining silent and submissive to men, avoiding ostentatious dress, and "clothing" themselves with good works, "as is proper for women who profess reverence for God" (I Timothy 2:9-13). Many biblical scholars have noted that this advice is inconsistent with much of what Paul said in his other letters. It is possible, then, that the author thought that women could accomplish more good through their example than by challenging expected behavior.

The author also says that women will be "saved" through childbirth. Many women would object that this statement characterizes them as nothing more than baby-making machines. But we have to be careful here. For while having children is certainly not all that women can do, it is still a vital role that they play in society. Moreover, when it is embraced as a calling from God, the path of motherhood certainly can be filled with heavenly grace and blessing.

We also hear that families should take care of their own. They are not to leave it to the church community to take care of their widows and orphans, and neither should they neglect their responsibilities to look after their needy family members. Again, this teaching is applicable today when many people ignore the plight of elderly or needy or ill members of their own families.

Finally, the author gives advice to slaves. They were to do their work without complaint, whether or not their owners were Christians. It is interesting that the author does not argue against slavery as an institution—it was an accepted reality of the time. There was very little that such a relatively marginal movement as early Christianity could have done to overturn such an entrenched institution. Although Christianity couldn't guarantee that it would improve the earthly condition of slaves in the short run (although it was largely responsible for its abolition in future generations), it offered them a guarantee of eternal life in the loving embrace of God. And through their example, no doubt many slaves converted their masters and secured better treatment, even if not always their freedom. The message for us today may be that no matter what work we are doing, we should do it respectfully and with dedication. We can give witness to our Christian values no matter what we are doing, as long as charity is our motivation.

Conclusion. In the following meditations, these themes and more will be explored, all with the goal of building up our sense of hope and expectancy for God's work in our lives and in the church at large. Many of the issues that Timothy faced so long ago continue to challenge us today, offering us countless opportunities to turn to the word of God for guidance and direction. What a comfort it is to know that people like Timothy and Paul have walked paths so similar to ours and have offered us so much God-inspired wisdom and hope!

1 Timothy 1:1-11

1 Paul, an apostle of Christ Jesus by the command of God our Savior and of Christ Jesus our hope,

2 To Timothy, my loyal child in the faith:

Grace, mercy, and peace from God the Father and Christ Jesus our Lord.

3 I urge you, as I did when I was on my way to Macedonia, to remain in Ephesus so that you may instruct certain people not to teach any different doctrine, 4and not to occupy themselves with myths and endless genealogies that promote speculations rather than the divine training that is known by faith. 5But the aim of such instruction is love that comes from a pure heart, a good conscience, and sincere faith. 6Some people have deviated from these and turned to meaningless talk, 7desiring to be teachers of the law, without understanding either what they are saying or the things about which they make assertions.

8 Now we know that the law is good, if one uses it legitimately. 9This means understanding that the law is laid down not for the innocent but for the lawless and disobedient, for the godless and sinful, for the unholy and profane, for those who kill their father or mother, for murderers, 10fornicators, sodomites, slave traders, liars, perjurers, and whatever else is contrary to the sound teaching 11that conforms to the glorious gospel of the blessed God, which he entrusted to me.

Have you ever had the experience of talking about Christianity with someone and ending up debating the latest popular book about Jesus that has come out? It may tell how the "hidden" books of the Bible reveal who Jesus "really" was—a very wise man who was in touch with special teachings but who was not necessarily divine. Or it may say that the essence of faith is really "self-actualization" and not self-emptying. Or maybe it tells how the tribulation period is upon us and that the end times are just around the corner. If you're not careful, you could end up having an argument instead of a conversation!

We've all experienced situations like this, and it's probably helpful to know that someone like Paul was there before us. The "myths and endless genealogies" and "speculations" that people were spreading in his day have a lot in common with what we find in our bookstores today. Both center on "secret" knowledge that looks attractive to people who are searching for the truth, but neither requires a truly changed life. Like fast food, they look tasty, but they don't offer anything of real substance.

Paul knew he could not ignore those who were promoting such erroneous ideas, because he had seen how their empty arguments could lure people away from Jesus. But he also knew from firsthand experience that these "vain discussions" could only be countered with the gospel. He was living proof that the most important—and radical—truth anyone would ever know was not an idea, but a person: Jesus Christ, the Son of God. Paul and the apostles did not have to follow "cleverly devised myths," for they were "eyewitnesses of his majesty" (2 Peter 1:16).

Like Timothy, we can and should be prepared to answer these false teachings. But our primary job is not to get into a debate. The most important thing we have to know is "Jesus Christ, and him crucified" (1 Corinthians 2:2). And knowing him means being transformed into his image. "Owe no one anything," Paul told the Romans, "except to love one another" (Romans 13:8). The only way our witness will convince others is if we give them the love that can change their lives. And what better way to love a skeptical world than by *being* the answer it is looking for!

"Lord, I ask for the grace to know your gospel and to *live* it. I want to be so transformed by you that my very life becomes a testament to who you are and what you can do in every person's life."

1 Timothy 1:12-17

[12] I am grateful to Christ Jesus our Lord, who has strengthened me, because he judged me faithful and appointed me to his service, [13]even though I was formerly a blasphemer, a persecutor, and a man of violence. But I received mercy because I had acted ignorantly in unbelief, [14]and the grace of our Lord overflowed for me with the faith and love that are in Christ Jesus. [15]The saying is sure and worthy of full acceptance, that Christ Jesus came into the world to save sinners—of whom I am the foremost. [16]But for that very reason I received mercy, so that in me, as the foremost, Jesus Christ might display the utmost patience, making me an example to those who would come to believe in him for eternal life. [17]To the King of the ages, immortal, invisible, the only God, be honor and glory forever and ever. Amen.

S t. Paul knew well his former way of life. He was not exaggerating when he said that he had been "a blasphemer, a persecutor, and a man of violence" (1 Timothy 1:13). All we have to do is read the story of his conversion in Acts 9 to get a glimpse of what he must have been like. And yet, by the power of God, he was transformed into an apostle and pastor who spread the gospel throughout the Middle East and Europe.

St. Philip Neri (1515–1595) was another person who was keenly aware of his sin and yet was a powerful servant of the Lord. As he turned to the Lord in prayer, Philip experienced an overflowing of grace and mercy to forgive and heal him. In time, he began to affect other people through his infectious joy over the love God had for him. Because he knew his own sins and his need for God's mercy so thoroughly, Philip became a compassionate confessor and an insightful pastor. Through this one man who knew the tremendous joy of redemption, God accomplished a spiritual renewal in the entire city of Rome.

Along with the gifts and talents we have received from the Lord, we also have our fair share of faults. The Holy Spirit wants to show us the truth about ourselves so that we will turn from our sins and receive God's mercy. We should never be afraid to ask the Spirit to reveal our sins to us. God-given insight into our spiritual needs will not paralyze us with introspection or low self-esteem. God wants to show us our own darkness only so that he can bring his light to bear more fully. Then we will become what the Lord wants us to be—men and women who have been freed from their sins and whose joy in their redemption affects everything they do and everyone they meet.

Do you want to make a difference in your family? In your parish? In your town? Get to know yourself, and get to know your Savior, who you need every day. When a Christian is filled with joy and peace, people can't help but be moved by his or her witness.

"Jesus, I want to know you more. Send the Spirit of truth to me, so that I may see my needs and faults. Cleanse me and help me enter more fully into your grace and mercy."

1 Timothy 1:18-20

[18] I am giving you these instructions, Timothy, my child, in accordance with the prophecies made earlier about you, so that by following them you may fight the good fight, [19]having faith and a good conscience. By rejecting conscience, certain persons have suffered shipwreck in the faith;[20]among them are Hymenaeus and Alexander, whom I have turned over to Satan, so that they may learn not to blaspheme.

What does it really mean to be a servant of God? Perhaps these few verses can give us some insight. Paul appreciated Timothy and his dedication to the gospel so much that he thought of him as his own child (1 Timothy 1:18). Very few people were as close to Paul or did as much for him as Timothy. When Paul needed a messenger, he often sent Timothy. When he wanted to learn how things were going in one of the churches he had founded, he sent Timothy. It's likely that Timothy spent some time in prison with Paul, and in several of Paul's letters, Timothy's name appears right next to his.

That's a pretty impressive record! Evidently, it wasn't what Timothy did, as much as who he was, that really endeared him to Paul. Listen to the "character reference" Paul gave when he told the Christians in

Philippi that he was sending Timothy to them: "I have no one like him who will be genuinely concerned for your welfare. All of them are seeking their own interests, not those of Jesus Christ. But Timothy's worth you know, how like a son with a father he has served with me in the work of the gospel" (Philippians 2:20-22).

Timothy was so valuable to Paul not because of his work ethic but because of the way he abandoned himself to Christ. In attitude, he followed the model of Jesus, the perfect Son, who "did not regard equality with God as something to be exploited, but emptied himself" (Philippians 2:6-7). Like Jesus, he held fast to God and to the Father's plan for his life, subordinating everything else to that plan.

To be a servant, then, is more about surrendering to God and trusting in what he wants to do with us than it is about exhausting ourselves trying to do all the right things. God has a beautiful blueprint for our lives—one that is exciting, fulfilling, and perfectly suited to the way we were created. "For we are what he has made us, created in Christ Jesus for good works, which God prepared beforehand to be our way of life" (Ephesians 2:10). Even the smallest act of kindness done in harmony with our calling is part of God's magnificent plan to unite all things in Christ. With an attitude like this, each of us can become deeply valuable servants advancing the kingdom of God.

"Father, I abandon myself to you. Let me be united to your wonderful plans for using me to reveal your love to the world. I only want to be your servant."

1 Timothy 2:1-7

[1] First of all, then, I urge that supplications, prayers, intercessions, and thanksgivings be made for everyone, [2]for kings and all who are in high positions, so that we may lead a quiet and peaceable life in all godliness and dignity. [3]This is right and is acceptable in the sight of God our Savior, [4]who desires everyone to be saved and to come to the knowledge of the truth. [5]For

there is one God;

there is also one mediator between God and humankind, Christ Jesus, himself human,

[6] who gave himself a ransom for all

—this was attested at the right time. [7]For this I was appointed a herald and an apostle (I am telling the truth, I am not lying), a teacher of the Gentiles in faith and truth.

Day after day, our newspapers and television screens show us the horrors of war, starvation, and suffering everywhere in the world; and even in our own countries, we learn of murder, drug addiction, poverty, and the killing of the unborn. We learn to put all this tragedy and sadness out of our minds and move on, somehow feeling separated or protected from these outrages against God's love.

Paul didn't feel this sense of separation or protection. When these words were written exhorting Timothy and his flock to pray for "kings and all who are in high positions, so that we may lead a quiet and peaceable life" (1 Timothy 2:2), a series of autocratic and often corrupt and evil Roman emperors had already passed through history. What faith the writer had in the power of prayer to transform lives! Through prayer, revelation, and experience, he had come to know that

God wants all people "to be saved and to come to the knowledge of the truth" (2:4).

So much did God desire this that he sent his Son to be the mediator between God and his people. By dying on the cross, Jesus paid the price that would allow all men and women to come into their rightful inheritance as children of God. Do we believe this truth or do we believe that God just wants to save a select few—those whom we love, those in our immediate circle of family and friends?

God wants us to pray for everyone—even those who hurt us the most. He wants us to pray for those who behave inhumanly; they are in the grip of this evil age and the prince of darkness.

To be effective in our prayer, we must first cleanse our hearts of hatred and unforgiveness and pray as Jesus taught us in the Lord's Prayer: "Forgive us our debts as we also have forgiven our debtors. . . ." (Matthew 6:12).

God's desire is that all people be saved and come to know the truth. He invites us to share in his divine desire by deciding to pray and intercede for the world on a regular basis. This invitation is a call to participate in his divine life. What a calling! What a privilege!

"Blessed Holy Spirit, open the eyes of those who are still blinded to the Father's love. Melt the hearts of those who are still cold to the salvation offered in Christ. Make us all into ambassadors of your grace and presence. Come, Holy Spirit, and renew the face of the earth!"

1 Timothy 2:8-15

[8] I desire, then, that in every place the men should pray, lifting up holy hands without anger or argument; [9]also that the women

should dress themselves modestly and decently in suitable clothing, not with their hair braided, or with gold, pearls, or expensive clothes, [10]but with good works, as is proper for women who profess reverence for God. [11]Let a woman learn in silence with full submission. [12]I permit no woman to teach or to have authority over a man; she is to keep silent. [13]For Adam was formed first, then Eve; [14]and Adam was not deceived, but the woman was deceived and became a transgressor. [15]Yet she will be saved through childbearing, provided they continue in faith and love and holiness, with modesty.

Doctors are always telling us that we need to pay attention to our hearts. Advertisements constantly remind us to monitor our cholesterol and blood pressure, and watch our diet and exercise habits. No matter how good we may look on the outside, they warn, we need to check these internal indicators of good health. While they are annoying, these messages have a point. After all, how can we ignore the most important organ we have?

Paul was making a similar point when he gave Timothy some advice about women's fashion. It may seem frivolous, or even chauvinistic, to us, but if we look closely at what Paul is doing here, we can detect a key underlying principle. By playing down extravagant clothes and "adornments," Paul sought to take the focus off appearances and get to the "heart" of the matter. Despite what some critics may say, Paul was not criticizing women for dressing up. The question he wanted them to ask was not "How do I look?" but "How do I look *to God?*"

The real "clothing" Paul was concerned with is far more elegant than anything we could buy at an upscale store. It's the fruit of holiness. Just like Peter, Paul wanted women to be clothed in "the inner self," and adorned with "the lasting beauty of a gentle and quiet spirit" (1 Peter 3:4). He wanted them to be clothed with the "good works" that flow from a heart surrendered to God in simple trust and faith. It's quite possible that Paul had in mind the ideal woman described in Proverbs 31—one who "opens her hand to the poor" and whose "clothing" is "strength and dignity" (Proverbs 31:20, 25). Paul would readily have agreed with the closing words of this passage: "Charm is deceitful, and beauty is vain, but a woman who fears the LORD is to be praised" (31:30).

No matter who we are—male or female, rich or poor—none of us can put on airs or fancy clothes to impress the Lord. He knows us inside and out. Perhaps we need to take a few moments to see what we are "wearing" today. Are we thankful and joyful for what God has given us? Do we have Jesus' heart of compassion and mercy for the people in our lives who are hard to deal with? Or are we carrying resentment or frustration? What is true of our physical health is even truer of our spiritual health. If we are to be healed, we need to be honest with the healer. Only then can he give us a "garment of praise" and use us for his work.

"Holy Spirit, cleanse my heart of anything that is displeasing to you. I want to be clothed in your glory, Lord!"

1 Timothy 3:1-7

[1] The saying is sure: whoever aspires to the office of bishop desires a noble task. [2]Now a bishop must be above reproach, married only once, temperate, sensible, respectable, hospitable, an apt teacher, [3]not a drunkard, not violent but gentle, not quarrelsome, and not a lover of money. [4]He must manage his own household well, keeping

his children submissive and respectful in every way—⁵for if some-one does not know how to manage his own household, how can he take care of God's church? ⁶He must not be a recent convert, or he may be puffed up with conceit and fall into the condemnation of the devil. ⁷Moreover, he must be well thought of by outsiders, so that he may not fall into disgrace and the snare of the devil.

Though Paul doesn't mention it by name, one of the most essen-tial qualities for a bishop to have is *humility*. It's easy, however, to be confused about what humility really means. In a worldly sense, it is usually associated with being submissive and mild-mannered. However, there is much more to humility than that—and mildness may not even be the foremost characteristic of the humble. More than any-thing else, humble people *know where they come from*. They are not arrogant because they know that they depend on God for absolutely everything—and that with him they can do absolutely anything.

St. Charles Borromeo (1538–1584) was definitely in the "humble" category. He became archbishop of Milan at the age of twenty-three—partly because of family connections and partly because of his considerable talents—but he never let that distinction go to his head. He had great power, but he seemed to care little for his position. He couldn't stand to be praised, and he once made a point of befriending a man who constantly criticized him! He fasted frequently and often slept in a chair. When the bubonic plague hit Milan in 1576, Borromeo not only ministered to the victims personally; he also gave up his own furnishings to help make some of the sufferers more com-fortable and hasten their recovery!

But while Borromeo seemed to care little about himself, he was by no means a quiet doormat. At a time when the church had grown corrupt, he became one of its most forceful reformers, both in his diocese of Milan and in the church as a whole. In his role as secretary of state for the Vatican, he instituted countless changes in all areas of Catholic life. He founded religious orders, seminaries, schools, hospitals, and shelters for the poor. He traveled long distances to make pastoral visits and correct abuses. Because he was a prayerful man, he seemed to carry Christ wherever he went. One of his friends said that his mere presence did more good than all the reforms he began.

As Borromeo's example shows us, true humility depends on our walk with the Lord. We can't fill up our schedules with ministry activities until we fill up our hearts with Jesus. Our goal is to be able to say with Paul, "It is no longer I who live, but it is Christ who lives in me" (Galatians 2:20). At the same time, however, humility will lead us to action. If we really believe that we are "a new creation," our focus will change from self-concern to a concern for God and his people. We'll be able to see with the eyes of Christ, and filled with the Holy Spirit, we will do what we were born to do—become saints!

"Lord, I can do nothing without you. Fill me with your grace, so that all I accomplish may be done in the power of your Spirit."

1 Timothy 3:8-13

8 Deacons likewise must be serious, not double-tongued, not indulging in much wine, not greedy for money; 9they must hold fast to the mystery of the faith with a clear conscience. 10And let them first be tested; then, if they prove themselves blameless, let them serve as deacons. 11Women likewise must be serious, not slanderers, but temperate, faithful in all things. 12Let deacons be married only

once, and let them manage their children and their households well; [13]for those who serve well as deacons gain a good standing for themselves and great boldness in the faith that is in Christ Jesus. ⟿

Paul's list of "dos and don'ts" for church leaders may seem tedious at first. It may be obvious to us, for instance, that deacons should be honest and sober. But we should remember that Paul didn't have it easy. Facing persecution from without and dissension within, there were times when he had to lay down the law. And come to think of it, things are not really all that different today. In the Western world, believers are often ridiculed for their faith, while in parts of Africa and Asia, Christians are persecuted and even put to death. Add to that the recent string of abuse scandals and arguments over church teaching, and you may end up with a scene very much like the challenges Paul and his companions faced two thousand years ago.

So what should we do? Follow the godly standards that Paul set out for Timothy to follow in Ephesus. As ambassadors for Christ, we should always strive to set a good example. After all, people are less likely to remember our words than our actions. As a case in point, the mention of Mother Teresa always brings a smile, even to people who say they don't believe in God. They may not know much about her religion, but they know what she did, as well as the peace, gentleness, and even joy with which she did it.

Following Paul's command to live righteously doesn't mean that we'll avoid all opposition. On the contrary, it's possible that we will even receive more. Remember what Jesus told his disciples: "If the world hates you, be aware that it hated me before it hated you" (John 15:18). Of course, since Jesus himself was put to death, then the closer we come to imitating him, the more we can expect opposition. But as

Peter writes, "it is better to suffer for doing good, if suffering should be God's will, than to suffer for doing evil" (1 Peter 3:17).

There's no mistake about it: Being godly can also be costly. However, the ultimate fulfillment of whatever we do in Christ will be to bring about his kingdom. We pray every day, "Thy kingdom come, thy will be done." Who can deny that in a world of darkness, his will is for us to "shine like stars in the world" (Phillippians 2:15) and so lead others to salvation? If this sometimes seems like an impossible task, let's remember that Jesus has already overcome the world for us, and that in living for him, we are "waiting for and hastening" his final coming (2 Peter 3:12)!

"Lord, I offer you my every action today. Let me be conscious of you always, so that I may not just talk the faith, but walk it!"

1 Timothy 3:14-16

[14] I hope to come to you soon, but I am writing these instructions to you so that, [15]if I am delayed, you may know how one ought to behave in the household of God, which is the church of the living God, the pillar and bulwark of the truth. [16]Without any doubt, the mystery of our religion is great:

He was revealed in flesh,
    vindicated in spirit,
        seen by angels,
proclaimed among Gentiles,
    believed in throughout the world,
        taken up in glory.

People have always been confronted with the question of what impact their faith should have on their daily lives. At the time the First Letter to Timothy was written, the fledgling church was exposed to many false teachers and deviant doctrines (1 Timothy 4: 1-10). There was much confusion, because many loud voices advocated conflicting beliefs and doctrinal positions. How was anyone to know how to live?

With all of the distractions of the modern world, we still confront the same question. We need to know "how one ought to behave in the household of God" (1 Timothy 3:15).

The First Letter to Timothy teaches that the church is founded upon the one, true, living God, "the pillar and bulwark of the truth" (1 Timothy 3:15). It is more than a building, a social structure, or a worldwide institution. It is a body brought together by God for the purpose of serving and glorifying him. In the church, the power, mercy, and love of God are made manifest to us. We as individuals are called to be a living part of this household, and our daily lives should reflect our inheritance as those who have been given life through Jesus Christ. We often presume that the gap between our human experience and heavenly realities is too great to be bridged. But 1 Timothy says that we *can* know how to conduct ourselves based upon what God has taught. We can live each day in faith, based upon the sure promises God holds out to us. The spiritual realities of the kingdom of God are made known to this earthly realm through his Son by the Spirit. If we allow God to teach us, we will know our inheritance as members of his household.

"Loving Father, give us the direction, guidance, grace, and strength to live this day as members of your household. Let your kingdom be manifested in our lives and in the lives of those around us."

1 Timothy 4:1-5

[1] Now the Spirit expressly says that in later times some will renounce the faith by paying attention to deceitful spirits and teachings of demons, [2]through the hypocrisy of liars whose consciences are seared with a hot iron. [3]They forbid marriage and demand abstinence from foods, which God created to be received with thanksgiving by those who believe and know the truth. [4]For everything created by God is good, and nothing is to be rejected, provided it is received with thanksgiving; [5]for it is sanctified by God's word and by prayer.

The difference between an optimist and a pessimist is like the difference between day and night. Optimists are upbeat, while pessimists seem almost naturally to focus on what's wrong. Optimists tend to be people of faith. They often see God working in apparently hopeless situations, while pessimists see only what's in front of them and worry about what they see. Optimists tend to count their blessings and give thanks for what they have, while pessimists tend to find fault and mourn what they are lacking.

When Paul warned about those who "forbid marriage and demand abstinence from foods" (1 Timothy 4:3), he was talking about some diehard pessimists who theologians today call "Gnostics" (from the Greek *gnosis*, which means "to know"). While there were many different groups in the first century that we might label Gnostics, most held that our earthly existence is like a prison. To them, the physical world was corrupt, and men and women were really "spiritual" beings trapped inside corrupt, "fleshly" bodies. They believed that humanity's salvation came through renouncing pleasure and acquiring esoteric, "spiritual" knowledge about the afterlife. Gnostics also reasoned that since the body was so vile, Jesus would never have become one of us. Instead, he only appeared to be human but was really only pure spirit.

As Paul explained to Timothy, the biggest error in such a philosophy was to miss that God himself is an optimist! From the beginning of creation, he has been on our side—even when we seemed to be beyond redemption. After he made us in his own image, "God saw everything that he had made, and indeed, it was very good" (Genesis 1:31). Even when we had fallen into sin, God still loved us enough and still held out enough hope that he willingly took on our nature and endured the cross just to redeem us. He didn't ask us to come to him first; he came to us. "God proves his love for us in that while we were still sinners Christ died for us" (Romans 5:8).

Accepting how much God loves us can help keep us from becoming twenty-first-century Gnostics. God created us to be a people of thanksgiving, who believe that the whole world is filled with the glory and grandeur of God. We don't have to try very hard to bring this attitude of blessing into a world that is so desperate for it. Every time we genuinely say "Praise the Lord!" or simply say "God bless you" to someone—every day that we show others a hopeful, optimistic spirit—we proclaim his glory. Just by enjoying God's presence within us, we can transmit his blessing to those who may never have known it.

"Lord, I praise you for your blessings! Bring me to those who need to believe in your goodness."

1 Timothy 4:6-11

⁶ If you put these instructions before the brothers and sisters, you will be a good servant of Christ Jesus, nourished on the words of the faith and of the sound teaching that you have followed. ⁷Have nothing to do with profane myths and old wives' tales. Train yourself in godliness, ⁸for, while physical training is of some value, godliness is valuable in every way, holding promise for both the present life and the life to come. ⁹The saying is sure and worthy of full acceptance. ¹⁰For to this end we toil and struggle, because we have our hope set on the living God, who is the Savior of all people, especially of those who believe.

¹¹ These are the things you must insist on and teach.

Train yourself in godliness. —1 Timothy 4:7

One morning when you are really busy at home, a neighbor calls with something on her mind. She talks, and talks, and talks—and you start to think about the time you are losing on those much-neglected chores. Finally, you get so annoyed that you cut her off in mid sentence and snap, "Excuse me but I have things to do!" After you hang up, you realize how impatient you were. "Oh, Lord," you sigh. "Please help me to be more patient."

These kinds of situations can often be part of our "training." When we think of spiritual "training," we might picture a seminarian studying for the priesthood, or a nun who prays for hours every day and practices rigorous self-denial. However, while prayer and penance are essential to spiritual development, the "daily grind" is the place where we are really stretched and given a chance to grow in grace.

And God has promised that he will give us that chance, by "pruning" every servant who bears fruit (John 15:2).

It is true that God is always using circumstances, both pleasant and unpleasant, to shape us into holy men and women. As one famous spiritual writer tells us, "There is not a moment in which God is not present with us under the cover of some pain to be endured, some obligation or some duty to be performed, or some consolation to be enjoyed. All that takes place within us, around us, or through us involves and conceals his divine hand" (Jean Pierre De Caussade, *The Joy of Full Surrender*).

So when Paul tells us to train *ourselves* in godliness, he is telling us to work hard at letting go of control! Many great athletes wouldn't have succeeded without submitting to the discipline of a coach. Like them, we too have to accept what God wants to do in our lives. He may allow us to suffer an illness or a job loss, or he may give us a great blessing that didn't exactly come the way we wanted. The Lord wants joyful disciples, and the most joyful are those who believe with all their hearts that "all things work together for good for those who love God" (Romans 8:28).

"Lord, I have often said yes, but still expected things to go my way. Today, let my yes be to everything you desire for me!"

1 Timothy 4:12-16

[12] Let no one despise your youth, but set the believers an example in speech and conduct, in love, in faith, in purity. [13]Until I arrive, give attention to the public reading of scripture, to exhorting, to teaching. [14]Do not neglect the gift that is in you, which was given to you

through prophecy with the laying on of hands by the council of elders. [15]Put these things into practice, devote yourself to them, so that all may see your progress. [16]Pay close attention to yourself and to your teaching; continue in these things, for in doing this you will save both yourself and your hearers.

Timothy was instructed to devote himself to reading Scripture, to exhortation and teaching, and to faithful completion of his duties. Particularly important was the call to progress in holiness in the way of Christ so that people might see God at work in his life and be encouraged by his example.

We may fail to see what instructions to leaders in the early church have to do with our lives today. Indeed, there is some debate over whether the letter was intended for Paul's disciple Timothy or if "Timothy" represents all leaders in the church. While the latter is more likely, in either case, the letter contains an important message for all Christian leaders and is analogous to God's calling for priests, deacons, religious, lay ministers, Christians with leadership responsibilities in the workplace, and parents.

The leaders' call to a holy way of life is closely linked to our calling. Even though our states in life are different, we are all called to progress in holiness. Just as Timothy was called to progress in understanding the Scriptures, we are also called to know God through his word. Leaders are to serve others humbly, and that humility begins with the recognition that God alone can give us wisdom to lead others. Thus, we need to seek God's wisdom on how to care for the body of Christ as manifested in our churches and families.

In addition, church leaders were called to exhort (preach) and teach: Preaching is recounting what is learned from God in Scripture;

teaching, on the other hand, involves caring for the body of believers, including children. Bishops, priests, and parents all have a responsibility to preach to and teach those under their care, especially those whose faith is weak or nonexistent.

We should not look upon the work God has entrusted to us as a burden or a task, but as intrinsic to our purpose in life.

"Heavenly Father, teach me to love your people as you do, and let that love be the basis of all I do. Give me wisdom through your word and help me to communicate that word to those in my care. Help me to pray for all those who are charged with responsibility for leadership in the body of Christ."

1 Timothy 5:1-16

[1] Do not speak harshly to an older man, but speak to him as to a father, to younger men as brothers, [2]to older women as mothers, to younger women as sisters—with absolute purity. [3] Honor widows who are really widows. [4]If a widow has children or grandchildren, they should first learn their religious duty to their own family and make some repayment to their parents; for this is pleasing in God's sight. [5]The real widow, left alone, has set her hope on God and continues in supplications and prayers night and day; [6]but the widow who lives for pleasure is dead even while she lives. [7]Give these commands as well, so that they may be above reproach. [8]And whoever does not provide for relatives, and especially for family members, has denied the faith and is worse than an unbeliever. [9] Let a widow be put on the list if she is not less than sixty years old and has been married only once; [10]she must be well attested for

her good works, as one who has brought up children, shown hospitality, washed the saints' feet, helped the afflicted, and devoted herself to doing good in every way. [11]But refuse to put younger widows on the list; for when their sensual desires alienate them from Christ, they want to marry, [12]and so they incur condemnation for having violated their first pledge. [13]Besides that, they learn to be idle, gadding about from house to house; and they are not merely idle, but also gossips and busybodies, saying what they should not say. [14]So I would have younger widows marry, bear children, and manage their households, so as to give the adversary no occasion to revile us. [15]For some have already turned away to follow Satan. [16]If any believing woman has relatives who are really widows, let her assist them; let the church not be burdened, so that it can assist those who are real widows.

. . . They should first learn their religious duty to their own family and make some repayment to their parents. . . . —1 Timothy 5:4

In a culture as disconnected as ours, it's not uncommon for parents and their grown children to become estranged. Even in healthy families, children may be so caught up in their jobs and their own families that they forget to give parents the love and affection they deserve.

But in this passage, Paul shows us how much God wants to see children stick by their parents, manifesting unconditional love and seventy-times-seven forgiveness, right to the end. It's true that some of us may feel so deeply wounded by our parents that it's impossible to love them as we ought. Many families have been wounded by events so painful that they wonder if there is any hope of reconciliation. There are also situations in which healing can come only gradually, after much prayer, patience, and time.

But no matter what our situation, we should never feel that God has rejected us or our parents. God didn't send his Son into the world to condemn, but to save (John 3:17). Jesus doesn't want to crush people with impossible laws or to tell them only where they may have gone wrong. He wants to meet all of us wherever we are in our life journey and offer us healing and restoration. God takes a special delight in turning the hearts of children to their parents and vice versa (Malachi 4:6).

So whatever your family situation, know that Jesus loves you just as much as ever. Know that he wants to mend the wounds between every father and son, mother and daughter. He wants to reconcile us, transform us, and use us to proclaim his kingdom—no matter what we have done in the past. Just as he did with the little children in the gospel, he wants to put his arms around us and give us his blessing (Mark 10:16).

Brothers and sisters, Jesus came "to proclaim release to the captives" (Luke 4:18). Through him, we can know greater and greater freedom from the strongholds of fear, mistrust, and hatred that have torn so many families apart. He comes to reconcile us not only to himself but also to each other—and that goes especially for our families. Let us trust in his power!

"Father, I bring my parents and my children before you. Through the blood you shed for us, I ask you to bring healing and forgiveness into our midst. May we love each other as you love us."

1 Timothy 5:17-25

¹⁷ Let the elders who rule well be considered worthy of double honor, especially those who labor in preaching and teaching; ¹⁸for the scripture says, "You shall not muzzle an ox while it is treading out the grain," and, "The laborer deserves to be paid." ¹⁹Never accept any accusation against an elder except on the evidence of two or three witnesses. ²⁰As for those who persist in sin, rebuke them in the presence of all, so that the rest also may stand in fear. ²¹In the presence of God and of Christ Jesus and of the elect angels, I warn you to keep these instructions without prejudice, doing nothing on the basis of partiality. ²²Do not ordain anyone hastily, and do not participate in the sins of others; keep yourself pure.

²³ No longer drink only water, but take a little wine for the sake of your stomach and your frequent ailments.

²⁴ The sins of some people are conspicuous and precede them to judgment, while the sins of others follow them there. ²⁵So also good works are conspicuous; and even when they are not, they cannot remain hidden.

Keep these instructions without prejudice, doing nothing on the basis of partiality. —1 Timothy 5:21

If we have any responsibility over other people, we may pause for a minute when we read these words. Paul is telling Timothy not to show favor to any human being when he makes a pastoral decision—especially when someone is accused of misconduct. Anyone who has been in this kind of situation—whether as a parent, a teacher, a pastor, or a catechist—knows how difficult it can be. We are human beings first and leaders second, and it's only natural to like one person better than another, to be afraid of offending someone, or to try to avoid confrontation if at all possible. So how can we avoid taking the easy way out?

We may find some help with this question by looking at the story of Susanna, found at the end of the Book of Daniel. Susanna, a young Jewish woman living in Babylon, was falsely accused of adultery by two elderly judges. The two men had actually tried to seduce her when she was alone in her husband's garden, but she refused. And in revenge, they brought trumped-up charges against her.

When these two judges tried to have Susanna put to death, God showed Daniel what they had really done. Daniel fearlessly defended Susanna and made the judges confess their guilt (Daniel 13).

When Susanna had the choice of giving in to the judges' seduction and threats, she had the courage to say, "I will fall into your hands, rather than sin in the sight of the Lord" (Daniel 13:23). Likewise, as one who studied the Scriptures, fasted, and prayed often, Daniel also had a deep relationship with the Lord. Susanna and Daniel triumphed because they had dedicated their lives to the Lord and placed their trust in him even in the most difficult of situations.

This story reveals two truths about leadership and tough choices. The first is that that *God knows the answer*. It is God who "knows what is in the darkness" (Daniel 2:22). And the second is that *we don't*. "Trust in the Lord with all your heart, and do not rely on your own insight" (Proverbs 3:5). Whether we are in charge of a company, a ministry, or a family, we can't make decisions based solely on appearance—especially when someone else's reputation is at stake. Like Daniel, we need to trust in the Holy Spirit, who "searches everything, even the depths of God" (1 Corinthians 2:10).

"Lord, help me to love you above anything or anyone else. May your Spirit always be my guiding light so that I will never judge others unfairly."

1 Timothy 6:1-5

¹ Let all who are under the yoke of slavery regard their masters as worthy of all honor, so that the name of God and the teaching may not be blasphemed. ²Those who have believing masters must not be disrespectful to them on the ground that they are members of the church; rather they must serve them all the more, since those who benefit by their service are believers and beloved.

Teach and urge these duties. ³Whoever teaches otherwise and does not agree with the sound words of our Lord Jesus Christ and the teaching that is in accordance with godliness, ⁴is conceited, understanding nothing, and has a morbid craving for controversy and for disputes about words. From these come envy, dissension, slander, base suspicions, ⁵and wrangling among those who are depraved in mind and bereft of the truth, imagining that godliness is a means of gain.

From these come envy, dissension, slander, base suspicions. . . .
—1 Timothy 6:4

All who teach in the name of our Lord Jesus—bishops, priests, ministers, deacons, religious, laypeople, even parents—have the responsibility to be good teachers. They must be firm and steadfast in the truth as well as faithful witnesses to the life, death, and resurrection of Christ.

The leaders of the early church had to deal constantly with false teachers and the damage they were doing. These spreaders of falsehood often appeared to be reasonable and well-meaning, but they didn't have God's truth as the source of their words; their deceptions threatened the unity of the church. Where false teaching exists, disputes, arguments, and controversies will eventually arise, leading to strife, envy, jealousy, and suspicion (1 Timothy 6:3-5). These are the work of the flesh that tend to weaken or fragment the body of Christ, rather than to unify it. False teaching is usually wrong in motive, source, and consequence.

It is important that the truth be taught accurately and lived faithfully if communities of believers are to grow and mature. When the truth is taught, it brings the light of Christ into situations, opening us to him who overcame sin, Satan, and the world. Good teachers will seek after righteousness in their own lives and guard the deposit of faith they have received. They will demonstrate those virtues that build up the body of Christ rather than vices that tear it down.

Let us examine our lives in light of the instructions to teachers in the First Letter to Timothy. Are we operating out of sound faith based on the truth which leads to eternal life? Is the fruit of the Spirit manifested in our words and in our lives? Are the things we say and the thoughts that underlie them based on the wisdom of Scripture, or are they the result of worldly wisdom and earthly precepts and values?

"Lord Jesus, may your Spirit work in my life and transform me. May the Spirit give me and all who are called to teach in your name clarity about the good news and the ability to share it with others."

1 Timothy 6:6-12

⁶Of course, there is great gain in godliness combined with contentment; ⁷for we brought nothing into the world, so that we can take nothing out of it; ⁸but if we have food and clothing, we will be content with these. ⁹But those who want to be rich fall into temptation

and are trapped by many senseless and harmful desires that plunge people into ruin and destruction. [10]For the love of money is a root of all kinds of evil, and in their eagerness to be rich some have wandered away from the faith and pierced themselves with many pains.

[11] But as for you, man of God, shun all this; pursue righteousness, godliness, faith, love, endurance, gentleness. [12]Fight the good fight of the faith; take hold of the eternal life, to which you were called and for which you made the good confession in the presence of many witnesses.

The love of money is the root of all kinds of evil. —1 Timothy 6:10

Through the centuries, Christians and non-Christians alike have recognized the dangers of loving money. Money, in itself, is not evil; many wealthy people have given generously of their resources out of love for God and neighbor. But the root of all evil is the *love* of money.

Love involves a wholehearted commitment of time and energy to serve the object of one's love. To love money is to desire it beyond need and reason, even to the point of obsession. This is why Jesus warned, "No one can serve two masters; for a slave will either hate the one and love the other, or be devoted to the one and despise the other. You cannot serve God and wealth" (Matthew 6:24).

Many Christians have lost the joy of being close to God as they pursued the riches of this world (1 Timothy 6:10). Nearly three centuries after the Letter to Timothy was written, St. John Chrysostom (c. 347–407), bishop of Constantinople, warned his congregation:

What evil is not caused by wealth, or rather not by wealth, but by the wicked will of those who do not know how to use it. . . .What fraudulent practices, what robberies! What miseries, enmities, contentions, battles! . . . Take away the love of money and you put an end to war, to battle, to enmity, to strife and contention. . . . The covetous man never knows a friend: a friend, did I say? He knows not God himself, driven mad, as he is, by the passion of avarice. (*Homilies on Timothy*, 17)

So what are we to do? The First Letter to Timothy teaches: "But as for you, man of God, shun all this; pursue righteousness, godliness, faith, love, endurance, gentleness" (1 Timothy 6:11). We are to shun the way of the world and seek the way of God. John Chrysostom put it this way: "Both expressions are emphatic; he does not say turn from one, and approach the other, but flee these things, pursue righteousness."

Like a competitor in a race, let us "fight the good fight of faith" and "take hold of the eternal life, to which [we] were called" through baptism (1 Timothy 6:12). As we fight the spiritual battle and take hold of the life of God and learn of his love, the grip money often has on our lives will be loosened, and our ability to use it properly will grow.

"Father, help me become as generous with my earthly resources as you are with your heavenly resources. I don't want to be possessed by my possessions but by you and you alone!"

1 Timothy 6:13-16

¹³ In the presence of God, who gives life to all things, and of Christ Jesus, who in his testimony before Pontius Pilate made the good confession, I charge you ¹⁴to keep the commandment without spot or blame until the manifestation of our Lord Jesus Christ, ¹⁵which he will bring about at the right time—he who is the blessed and only Sovereign, the King of kings and Lord of lords. ¹⁶It is he alone who has immortality and dwells in unapproachable light, whom no one has ever seen or can see; to him be honor and eternal dominion. Amen.

Paul gave Timothy a great and noble commission: He was to serve the Lord, "without spot or blame" (1 Timothy 6:14). Perhaps like all those who are keenly aware of their own inadequacies, Timothy felt overwhelmed by this charge. Yet Paul delivered this directive "in the presence of God who gives life to all things, and of Christ Jesus" (6:13). Paul himself knew what it was like to experience God's presence, and so he was confident in the Lord's ability to empower Timothy to serve him—in spite of Timothy's weaknesses and failings.

On the way to Damascus, Paul experienced the presence of Jesus in such a powerful way that it transformed his entire life (Acts 9:1-22). From that encounter, Paul became not only a loyal follower of Jesus, but also a great evangelist who willingly suffered shipwrecks and imprisonment for God. Moses met the living God in a burning bush. Through God's presence, he was empowered to confront the pharaoh and lead his people out of slavery, even though he did not think that he could do it (Exodus 3:1-12; 5:1).

Both Paul and Moses—and so many others—show us how life-changing an experience of the Lord's presence can be. Like a warm blanket, God covers us with a love that startles and overwhelms us by its intensity. It clothes us in peace and protects us in trials. It is a love that cries out for a response from us, and only our most precious gift—the offering of our entire lives—seems worthy of the King of Kings.

By virtue of our baptism, God has given us the same commission that Paul gave to Timothy. But to carry it out, we must draw our strength from the Lord. We cannot do it on our own. Do you seek the Lord's presence every day in prayer? Do you know the Holy Spirit's work of comforting and directing you? God will come to you if you open your heart to him. Let us take up his holy invitation and welcome him into our lives.

"Jesus, I want to experience your presence. Though I am a sinner, you have redeemed me by your cross and resurrection. Come into my life in a powerful way so that I may carry out your work on earth."

1 Timothy 6:17-21

[17] As for those who in the present age are rich, command them not to be haughty, or to set their hopes on the uncertainty of riches, but rather on God who richly provides us with everything for our enjoyment. [18] They are to do good, to be rich in good works, generous, and ready to share, [19] thus storing up for themselves the treasure of a good foundation for the future, so that they may take hold of the life that really is life.

[20] Timothy, guard what has been entrusted to you. Avoid the profane chatter and contradictions of what is falsely called knowledge; [21] by professing it some have missed the mark as regards the faith.

Grace be with you.

Guard what has been entrusted to you. —*1 Timothy 6:20*

I magine Paul writing the last lines of this letter. Perhaps he is thinking of his amazing conversion on the road to Damascus, and the revelation he received there of God's love and mercy. From that moment on, he spent the rest of his life trying to pass on the message of salvation. The last thing he wanted was to see a church that he helped found lose its flame of excitement, devotion, and desire for the Lord. And so his final words are a plea to Timothy to hold on to the precious treasure that he has been "entrusted" with.

Long before the church of Ephesus was even founded, this "deposit of faith" that was entrusted to Timothy was present in the preaching of the apostles. Over the years, it took root in the Scriptures and the sacred tradition that we have inherited. This "deposit" is not any one thing, but it includes the whole package: all of the church's teachings, all of the teachings of her bishops, all the witness of her saints—all working hand in hand with the inspired word of God to reach the world with the message of salvation.

Paul knew that the driving force of faith rested not in the Bible or in sermons or in volumes of church documents, but in the Holy Spirit who makes all of these elements come to life for us. Without the Spirit's guidance, the church would still be debating the divinity of Jesus, justification by faith, and a number of other vital issues. We can be thankful for Jesus' promise that the Holy Spirit will teach us everything and remind us of all that he said (John 14:26).

As you reflect gratefully on the heritage of the church, remember that Paul's letter is addressed to you as much as to Timothy. Each of us is a well-honored heir of the faith. All the glorious riches of the gospel belong to us. There is one condition, however: We are called to share our wealth with others. Jesus assures us that if we do, our faith will only grow richer. "To all those who have, more will be given" (Luke 19:26). There is a good chance that someone is waiting for the spiritual blessings we've been holding on to. May we not miss any opportunity to be just as generous with others as Jesus has been with us!

"Lord, I praise you for the greatness of the faith I have inherited from your first followers. Give me the wisdom and love I need to impart this same faith to everyone you have placed in my life."

Paul's Last Will and Testament

The Second Letter to Timothy

PAUL'S LAST WILL AND TESTAMENT

Paul's Last Will and Testament
An Introduction to the Second Letter to Timothy

by Fr. George Montague, SM

Written under the shadow of the Roman sword that will claim his life, Paul's Second Letter to Timothy is clearly the last of the so-called pastoral epistles. Many commentaries have also called it Paul's last will and testament or his farewell discourse. It parallels in letter form what Luke presents in narrative form in Acts 20:17-35, which recounts Paul's address to the elders of Ephesus.

St. Paul or a Successor? But who is this "Paul" of the pastorals? The earliest references to these letters all assume that they are from Paul of Tarsus, the apostle who wrote the major New Testament letters to the Romans, Corinthians, and Galatians (which today are referred to as the "undisputed letters"). The only exception to these ancient witnesses was the second-century Marcion, otherwise a champion of Paul, who rejected the pastorals as neither inspired nor written by Paul— probably because they disagreed with his own heretical views.

It was only in the early nineteenth century that the German scholar Friedrich Schleiermacher questioned the authenticity of 1 Timothy on the basis of its vocabulary. Schleiermacher's questionings opened the gate to a position ultimately held by most modern scholars who doubt that Paul actually wrote any of the pastorals. Instead, these scholars hold that they were written after Paul's death by someone standing in the tradition of Paul to address the concerns of a later-generation church. In this view, even the Timothy and Titus of the letters themselves are not historical persons but models or types of later church leadership.

This position, which is held today even by many Catholic scholars, does not deny the inspired nature of these letters. In biblical times, attributing a work to a great authority of the past was not unusual. For example, many of the psalms were attributed to David, even though he may have written only a few, if any. Works of the wisdom tradition were attributed to Solomon. And Chapters 40 to 55 of the Book of Isaiah are the work of a poet-prophet living over a hundred years after the historical Isaiah.

However, this widespread approach to the pastorals is itself being questioned by more recent scholars who are returning to the traditional view that they belong to the apostle Paul. These scholars point out that the differences from the other letters can be explained by evidence that was initially overlooked; by the fact that these are letters to individuals rather than to a whole community; and by considering that the subject matter covered in these letters is quite different from the ones written to entire communities.

Whoever wrote these letters, we do know that believers as far back as the second century believed that they had been written by Paul—even as they questioned the authorship of other letters (like Hebrews) for some time. This means that from the beginning, the church was hearing the pastorals as part of the authentic apostolic tradition, and therefore as the inspired word of God. So in order to help us better understand the message of the Second Letter to Timothy, let us enter into the world of its two principal characters: Paul and Timothy.

Paul: A Pastor in Chains. Paul is in prison in Rome. The city's prisons varied in severity; the worst was the Mamertine prison, which consisted of only two rooms made of tufa rock. The lower room for the prisoners, about thirty feet in diameter, was accessible only from a hole in the ceiling. The upper room was for the guards. Like other Roman prisons, it would have been bitterly cold in winter. But since Paul can receive visitors, even though he is in chains (perhaps chained to a Roman soldier?), it seems that his confinement was what was called *custodia militaris*, military custody. He was, after all, a Roman citizen.

What is Paul feeling at this moment? Very much like Jesus, he is troubled not so much at the probability of his own death—"whether we live or whether we die, we are the Lord's" (Romans 14:8)—for he knows that the crown of righteousness awaits him (2 Timothy 4:8). His deeper feeling is loneliness and lack of support even from some of his own disciples. "Only Luke is with me," he writes (4:11). He has been deserted by his disciples Phygelus and Hermogenes (1:15), by Demas, "in love with this present world" (4:10), and by everyone at the moment on his first defense (4:16).

Thus he asks Timothy to come to him as soon as possible, bringing the cloak that Paul had left in Troas (2 Timothy 4:13), and to do so before winter (4:21). Two reasons prompt this request: Paul will need the cloak to endure the coming cold weather; and sailing was very treacherous, nearly impossible, during winter. He did experience one consolation, however, in the visit of Onesiphorus, who came to Rome and searched for Paul until he found him. This faithful friend helped Paul in many ways and "was not ashamed of my chain" (1:16-17). Onesiphorus' bravery may even have cost him his life, for Paul's words of high praise (1:16-18) and his request that he be remembered to his household (4:19) may suggest that he has died.

Paul's personal survival and comfort is not his primary concern, however, nor the reason for this letter. If we can sense Paul's intense affection for Timothy—"my beloved child" (2 Timothy 1:2)—we can sense even more strongly his concern that the treasure entrusted to Timothy be carried on. What is at issue is the *apostolic tradition*. In Paul's view, this pure and healthy doctrine was being threatened not so much by persecution as by false teachings. Already in 1 Corinthians 15:1-2 Paul had said that the gospel will save only if it is kept exactly as he had preached it. But in this letter, the concern for orthodoxy becomes paramount: Paul fears the loss of the tradition more than the loss of his own life! This means that Timothy must do more than hold fast to the tradition himself (2 Timothy 1:13) and vigorously preach it whether convenient or not (4:2). He must also form others who can do so and who in turn can teach it to even more people (2:2).

Paul especially warns against frivolous "disputes" that do not promote holiness (2 Timothy 2:14-19). An example is the reference to Hymenaeus and Philetus, who are teaching that the resurrection has already taken place (2:18). However much Paul had earlier taught that the seed of resurrection had been planted in every Christian heart, he knows that the full resurrection lies ahead: "If we have died with him, we will also live with him" (2:11). In Christ physical death has been disabled, robbed of its power, and made ineffective because of the life and immortality revealed in the gospel (1:10).

New Challenges for Timothy. All of this is a message that Timothy himself needs to hear, for he appears to be in a crisis of discouragement. When Paul says that he remembers Timothy's tears, he is likely referring to the wrenching moment when the imperial police arrested and took his mentor, Paul, away from the young man (2 Timothy 1:4). Paul's arrest left Timothy shaken and perhaps less bold in his proclamation of Christ, for Paul has to tell him not to "be ashamed, then, of the testimony about our Lord or of me his prisoner" (1:8). Timothy seems earlier to have been tempted to leave Ephesus to go either with

Paul or to other mission fields, but Paul told him to stay put (1 Timothy 1:3).

"Be strong," Paul urges, "in the grace that is in Christ Jesus" (2 Timothy 2:1). He tells Timothy to fan into flame the grace that is in him by his ordination at Paul's hands: "For God did not give us a spirit of cowardice, but rather a spirit of power and of love and of self-discipline" (1:7). It is a message given to all who feel the weight of their vocation and need a renewal of their initial enthusiasm in the Lord's service. It also speaks to the reality of sacramental grace—a grace that can be stirred up and grow ever brighter on the journey of discipleship and mission.

It is to this letter that we also owe the strongest affirmation that all of Scripture is divinely inspired and useful "for teaching, for reproof, for correction, and for training in righteousness" (2 Timothy 3:16). "Inspired" here means literally, "breathed by God." Whatever its human authorship, Scripture is the word of God. The Scriptures here refer to what we call the Old Testament, but by this time the words of Jesus were being recorded, and these were understood to have the same divine authority, even greater, than the Jewish Scriptures or the Septuagint. Before being assembled in the gospels, they were doubtless circulating in the Christian communities, for Paul refers to Jesus' words to give authority to his own teaching (1 Corinthians 7:10,12). He may very well be referring to such *testimonia* when he tells Timothy to bring with him "the books, and above all the parchments" (2 Timothy 4:13).

As is typical of farewell discourses, Paul warns of hard times to come (2 Timothy 3:1-9). Jesus had done so in the apocalyptic sections of the synoptic gospels and in the Last Supper discourse in John. And in his farewell speech to the elders from Ephesus, Paul had warned of "wolves" that would ravage the flock (Acts 20:29-30). But Paul still has hope that God will give the grace of repentance to the opponents of his gospel and that they will be freed from the devil's snare that has entrapped them (2 Timothy 2:26).

An interesting sidelight emerges from the attention Paul gives to Timothy's grandmother and mother, from whom Timothy first learned the faith (2 Timothy 1:5). The apostolic tradition will be handed on not only by Paul to Timothy and by Timothy to other teachers (2:2). It will be carried on by faithful women like grandma Lois (Paul uses the familiar title) and mother Eunice, who will train the next generation. Clearly, Paul recognized that the life of faith lives in the community of the believers. Theologians call it the *sensus fidelium*, the perception or consciousness or manner of thinking of the faithful at large, who know the faith by living it. Men or women, they have a share, under the pastoral guidance of the bishops, in passing on the gospel in all its strength and purity.

Neither Death Nor Life . . . Finally, we cannot fail to be moved by Paul's final testament. He may be in chains, but the word of God is not (2 Timothy 2:9). His life is a libation already being poured out; he has finished the race, and he now awaits the crown (4:6-8). Paul may not have been an athlete, but he knew the Greeks too well to overlook their love of sports. He often uses the metaphor of a race, and at least once he used the image of boxing to describe the *agon*, the struggle in this life to win the crown of the next.

Nero may have his day when the executioner beheads Paul; but it is also Paul's day as he walks confidently to the block to bear witness that "if we have died with him, we will also live with him" (2 Timothy

2:11). In his letter to the Roman Christians much earlier, Paul had asked rhetorically whether anything could separate the faithful from the love of Christ. He listed a number of things, the last of which was *the sword* (Romans 8:35). Ironically, it was in Rome and by an imperial sword, as tradition has it, that he would give his life for his Lord. His fidelity to his call and his mission would bear witness to what he had also written to the Romans: "I am convinced that neither death nor life . . . nor rulers . . . nor anything else in all creation will be able to separate us from the love of God in Christ Jesus our Lord" (8:38-39).

Paul's Last Will and Testament

2 Timothy 1:1-6

[1] Paul, an apostle of Christ Jesus by the will of God, for the sake of the promise of life that is in Christ Jesus,

[2] To Timothy, my beloved child:

Grace, mercy, and peace from God the Father and Christ Jesus our Lord.

[3] I am grateful to God—whom I worship with a clear conscience, as my ancestors did—when I remember you constantly in my prayers night and day. [4]Recalling your tears, I long to see you so that I may be filled with joy. [5]I am reminded of your sincere faith, a faith that lived first in your grandmother Lois and your mother Eunice and now, I am sure, lives in you. [6]For this reason I remind you to rekindle the gift of God that is within you through the laying on of my hands; . . .

Rekindle the gift of God that is within you. —2 Timothy 1:6

One of the best ways we can rekindle God's gift within us is to recall in prayer the truth of the gospel we have received. God has saved us and called us to a holy life—not because of any merit of ours, but because of his tremendous love for us. Even before the world began, he determined that he would extend his grace to all men and women through Jesus Christ (Ephesians 1:4). By his cross, Jesus has robbed death of its powerful sting and has brought life and immortality to us through the gospel. Now we can receive all the grace that God intended for us from the beginning. All that God expects of us, he gives to us in his Son through the power of the Holy Spirit.

71

Often, we find ourselves wanting to pray, but cannot seem to find the time. We want to love others, but we sometimes become impatient and say or do things we later regret. We try hard to do the right things, but events and situations don't always turn out the way we planned. Where can we go for help? Who can help us with our shortcomings?

As with everything else, Jesus is the answer to our need. He can do in us the very things that we are powerless to do on our own. Because he has sent his Spirit to dwell within us, his grace is ever available. He has broken the power of sin and called us to place our faith and our trust in him. Through faith in Christ, we become reconciled with our Father in heaven and empowered to live holy lives as his beloved children.

We received the seed of this faith when we were baptized. Everything we need to walk in God's ways is within us. Let us come to know the grace of Jesus as we tend to that seed—as we nurture the faith within us. How do we help the seed of our faith grow and mature? Nothing dramatic is required, only daily attention. We can set aside a little time for daily prayer, ponder the Scriptures, focus on a truth or promise of God, and quiet our hearts during Mass. Let us open our hearts to the Spirit and light of the gospel.

"Jesus, we believe that you alone have the power to take away our sins and grant us life. Give us hearts that treasure the gospel so that your love may be manifested to the world."

2 Timothy 1:7-14

[7][F]or God did not give us a spirit of cowardice, but rather a spirit of power and of love and of self-discipline.

[8] Do not be ashamed, then, of the testimony about our Lord or of

me his prisoner, but join with me in suffering for the gospel, relying on the power of God, [9]who saved us and called us with a holy calling, not according to our works but according to his own purpose and grace. This grace was given to us in Christ Jesus before the ages began, [10]but it has now been revealed through the appearing of our Savior Christ Jesus, who abolished death and brought life and immortality to light through the gospel. [11]For this gospel I was appointed a herald and an apostle and a teacher, [12]and for this reason I suffer as I do. But I am not ashamed, for I know the one in whom I have put my trust, and I am sure that he is able to guard until that day what I have entrusted to him. [13]Hold to the standard of sound teaching that you have heard from me, in the faith and love that are in Christ Jesus. [14]Guard the good treasure entrusted to you, with the help of the Holy Spirit living in us.

A priest advises a man who comes to him for confession to think about football. Evidently, the man has begun to feel discouraged because he can't see much progress in overcoming a certain pattern of sin. The priest tells him to remember how, in a football game, you have to focus your attention on getting the ball, but that getting the ball doesn't end the game. There will be other times when the ball will come your way. Even if you miss, the game doesn't end. You have to go after the ball again and again and again.

Doesn't this sound like Paul's advice to Timothy? Writing from prison in Rome, Paul urged the young apostle to shake off discouragement and go on with the game. Like a good team captain, he reassured Timothy that he had what he needed to keep the faith and pass it on to others: "God did not give us a spirit of cowardice, but rather a spirit of power and of love and of self-discipline" (2 Timothy 1:7).

The Holy Spirit was greater than any personal weaknesses that might be eroding Timothy's work!

Ironically, Paul may have looked defeated, since he was in prison. But he turned Timothy's attention back to a true perspective—the perspective of the gospel. It was Paul's and Timothy's job to keep their eyes on the ball and their minds on their calling, since God gave it to them—and us—"not according to our works but according to his own purpose" (2 Timothy 1:9). The good news is that we are on the winning team, with a captain who keeps cheering us on.

Sure, we sometimes feel defeated, confused, and frustrated. We get down on ourselves for not making every play. But let's remember that Jesus has already won our salvation. Now he calls us to serve him, not so that we will earn a place in heaven, but because we want to see other people filled with the same love that has filled us. Take Paul's advice and "rekindle the gift of God that is within you" (2 Timothy 1:6). Keep your eye on the ball, and you will pass the good news on to others.

"Jesus, thank you for winning my salvation through your death and resurrection. Help me stay focused on the truth of your love for me."

2 Timothy 1:15-18

15 You are aware that all who are in Asia have turned away from me, including Phygelus and Hermogenes. 16May the Lord grant mercy to the household of Onesiphorus, because he often refreshed me and was not ashamed of my chain; 17when he arrived in Rome, he eagerly searched for me and found me—18may the Lord grant that he will find mercy from the Lord on that day! And you know very well how much service he rendered in Ephesus.

What contrasting portraits emerge in these few short verses! The defection of Phygelus and Hermogenes—as well as Paul's abandonment by others in Asia—sharply contrasts with the loyalty and devotion of Onesiphorus. Thus, with just a few telling lines, Paul sketched a striking study of the difference between false and true friendship.

Paul's reference to Phygelus and Hermogenes—the only information about them the New Testament provides—suggests that they were "fair weather" friends. Perhaps they had feared that associating with someone who landed in jail so often had become just too dangerous. Maybe they had expected Christianity to be a lot easier than it turned out to be. Or maybe they simply decided that Paul wasn't worth their loyalty and wanted to find another leader to follow who wasn't as demanding—as if Christianity were focused upon the people who ran churches and not the Lord who died to bring about the church!

By contrast, Onesiphorus had "often refreshed" Paul, encouraging and comforting him. Unashamed to be known as Paul's friend, he had even searched Rome to find the apostle, who was most likely in prison or under house arrest (2 Timothy 1:16). We can't help but wonder if Onesiphorus realized that he was fulfilling Jesus' words, "I was in prison and you visited me. . . . Just as you did it to one of the least of these who are members of my family, you did it to me" (Matthew 25:36, 40).

What proof of genuine love it is when one willingly endures difficulties for a friend and shares in his or her sufferings! "Friendship heightens the joys of prosperity and mitigates the sorrows of adversity by dividing and sharing them," wrote St. Aelred of Rievaulx (1109–1167) in his famous treatise *Spiritual Friendship*. "Hence, the best medicine in life is a friend." His words echo those of the Hebrew sage Ben Sira: "Faithful friends are beyond price; no amount can balance their worth. Faithful friends are life-saving medicine" (Sirach 6:15-16).

In Onesiphorus Paul was blessed with just the kind of friend described by Aelred and Ben Sira.

This passage offers us an opportunity to take a look at our own friendships. Are there people in our lives like Onesiphorus? People who would go through fire for us? They are the true treasures of our lives, and we should honor them and thank God for them every day. Similarly, are there people who we would go out of our way to serve and care for? Perhaps today would be a good day to reaffirm the value of friendship in our lives and to ask God's special blessing upon our closest relationships.

" 'No one has greater love than this, to lay down one's life for one's friends' (John 15:13). Jesus, help me to follow your example and love others as you have loved me."

2 Timothy 2:1-7

¹ You then, my child, be strong in the grace that is in Christ Jesus; ²and what you have heard from me through many witnesses entrust to faithful people who will be able to teach others as well. ³Share in suffering like a good soldier of Christ Jesus. ⁴No one serving in the army gets entangled in everyday affairs; the soldier's aim is to please the enlisting officer. ⁵And in the case of an athlete, no one is crowned without competing according to the rules. ⁶It is the farmer who does the work who ought to have the first share of the crops. ⁷Think over what I say, for the Lord will give you understanding in all things.

Runners train hard to get into top physical condition when they're preparing for a big race. They willingly endure the discipline, long hours of practice, diet restrictions, fatigue—even pain—that their training entails. In all these things, they are willing to push beyond their normal limits in the hopes of winning. Then, during the race itself, all their energies are fixed on crossing the finish line: Victory is the reward for all their effort.

Paul frequently used images from athletics in his advice to the young Christian churches. To the believers in Corinth, he wrote: "Run in such a way that you may win [the prize]. Athletes exercise self-control in all things; they do it to receive a perishable wreath, but we an imperishable one" (1 Corinthians 9:24-25). Similarly, he explained to the Philippians that "forgetting what lies behind and straining forward to what lies ahead, I press on toward the goal for the prize of the heavenly call of God in Christ Jesus" (Philippians 3:13-14). So when Timothy needed encouragement to bear the hardships that were an inevitable part of living the gospel, Paul reminded him that "no one is crowned without competing according to the rules" (2 Timothy 2:5). In other words, Paul was exhorting Timothy to trust God and remain steadfast and obedient to his call. That's how he could avoid being disqualified from the contest. Ultimately, it's also the way he'd win the prize.

Paul knew that Timothy faced many challenges in his ministry in Ephesus, so he urged him to "be strong in the grace that is in Christ Jesus" and put up with suffering for the sake of the gospel (2 Timothy 2:1, 3). We, too, can be sure that struggles and sufferings will come our way as we live the gospel and share it with others. Being faithful to the Lord demands discipline and sacrifice. But just as Paul's words strengthened Timothy's resolve to persevere, they have the same power today to inject new heart into us as we follow the Lord. If we reflect on his advice, "the Lord will give [us] understanding in all things" (2:7).

Winning a race requires every ounce of a runner's strength. If an athlete works so hard to gain passing glory, how much more should we be willing to put our whole effort into winning the crown of righteousness (2 Timothy 4:8). So let's stay the course!

"Father, help me to 'run with perseverance the race that is set before me, looking to Jesus the pioneer and perfecter of my faith' (Hebrews 12:1-2)."

2 Timothy 2:8-13

8   Remember Jesus Christ, raised from the dead, a descendant of David—that is my gospel, 9for which I suffer hardship, even to the point of being chained like a criminal. But the word of God is not chained. 10Therefore I endure everything for the sake of the elect, so that they may also obtain the salvation that is in Christ Jesus, with eternal glory. 11The saying is sure:

If we have died with him, we will also live with him;
12   if we endure, we will also reign with him;
if we deny him, he will also deny us;
13   if we are faithless, he remains faithful—
for he cannot deny himself.

Remember Jesus Christ, raised from the dead . . . that is my gospel.
—2 Timothy 2:8

Jesus' resurrection was the keynote of Paul's preaching, the crux of the gospel he proclaimed so zealously and for which he endured hardship, imprisonment, and even the threat of death. The resurrection of Christ has been called the epicenter of Christianity, the climax and crowning truth of faith, the foundation of human destiny, and the promise of the world to come. The entire Christian faith can be summed up in three simple words: "Christ is risen."

Through Jesus' death and resurrection, we "obtain salvation in Christ Jesus, with eternal glory" (2 Timothy 2:9-10). Not only have we been redeemed from bondage to sin here and now, we have also been given hope in the face of death. Although every human being must still die, the grave is not the end. Jesus decisively conquered death so that we can be raised up to immortality with him.

During the repression of religion in Russia in the early twentieth century, a Bolshevik commissar in charge of education attacked the "outdated" faith of Christian believers. Gathering the people together in the Polytechnic Museum, he gave a presentation denouncing Christianity. Feeling confident that he had done a convincing job of exposing the falsehood of the resurrection, he offered the podium to anyone who might wish to offer a rebuttal or engage in a brief dialogue.

An Orthodox priest came forward. Looking at the priest in disdain, the official said, "You have five minutes." The priest agreed to be brief. Climbing the speaker's platform, he suddenly threw his hands into the air and shouted at the top of his lungs, "Brothers and sisters, Christ is risen!" The crowd unhesitatingly thundered back as with one voice, "Christ is risen indeed!"

Jesus' resurrection is not simply a historical event in the ancient past that is now irrelevant to us. Its implications and effects extend from the first Easter morning to today and beyond, through all eternity. Jesus, once dead, lives again! "The saying is sure: If we have died with him, we will also live with him" (2 Timothy 2:11).

"Jesus, you are the risen Lord, exalted in glory! In you, we too are raised up! In you, we too share in eternal life!"

2 Timothy 2:14-19

14   Remind them of this, and warn them before God that they are to avoid wrangling over words, which does no good but only ruins those who are listening. 15Do your best to present yourself to God as one approved by him, a worker who has no need to be ashamed, rightly explaining the word of truth. 16Avoid profane chatter, for it will lead people into more and more impiety, 17and their talk will spread like gangrene. Among them are Hymenaeus and Philetus, 18who have swerved from the truth by claiming that the resurrection has already taken place. They are upsetting the faith of some. 19But God's firm foundation stands, bearing this inscription: "The Lord knows those who are his," and, "Let everyone who calls on the name of the Lord turn away from wickedness."

Words can be a potent force for good or evil. There is tremendous power in what we say and in what we listen to: "Death and life are in the power of the tongue" (Proverbs 18:21). We can bring clarity, peace, and encouragement to those around us by prudently speaking words that are true and sensible. We can also sow dissension, controversy, and unrest by carelessly speaking words that are false or foolish.

It seems that imprudent and misleading speech was upsetting the young church at Ephesus. Some were "wrangling over words" (2 Timothy 2:14), which probably meant that controversies or gossip were taking the place of love and honor for the gospel and for one another. Idle and worldly chatter was spreading "like gangrene" through the body of believers, causing at least two influential members to embrace faulty teachings about the resurrection (2:16-18). It seems that some subtle arguments had reduced the promise of a future bodily resurrection to a spiritual "experience" at baptism, thus undermining the faith of some of the members of the community. No wonder Paul urged Timothy to "rightly explain the word of truth" (2:15)!

In the original Greek of Paul's letter, the expression "rightly explain" literally means "to cut or keep a straight course" as, for example, in the way a farmer plows a straight furrow or a mason builds a straight wall. Thus, Timothy was to preach the gospel straightforwardly—that is, in a clear and direct way that everyone could understand. It was Timothy's responsibility as a teacher and pastor to teach the gospel to the Ephesians in a way that protected the certainties of the Christian faith.

Sadly, Paul's description of the profane talk, false teaching, and senseless speculation going on in ancient Ephesus sounds familiar today. Every day, we are offered subjective versions of truth that misrepresent the gospel. Every day, we have to sort through numerous opinions—even the ones inside our own minds—that have the potential of undermining the calling we've received. Just as Paul exhorted Timothy, we too need to be careful in discerning what we take in.

"Holy Spirit, guide me in your truth. Form my heart and mind by the 'sound words of our Lord Jesus Christ and the teaching that is in accordance with godliness' (1 Timothy 6:3)."

2 Timothy 2:20-26

20 In a large house there are utensils not only of gold and silver but also of wood and clay, some for special use, some for ordinary. 21All who cleanse themselves of the things I have mentioned will become special utensils, dedicated and useful to the owner of the house, ready for every good work. 22Shun youthful passions and pursue righteousness, faith, love, and peace, along with those who call on the Lord from a pure heart. 23Have nothing to do with stupid and senseless controversies; you know that they breed quarrels. 24And the Lord's servant must not be quarrelsome but kindly to everyone, an apt teacher, patient, 25correcting opponents with gentleness. God may perhaps grant that they will repent and come to know the truth, 26and that they may escape from the snare of the devil, having been held captive by him to do his will.

Pursue righteousness, faith, love, and peace. —2 Timothy 2:22

What a lifetime program! Paul encouraged Timothy to foster these Christlike qualities in his life so that everyone around him—whether they were Christians, Jews, or pagans—would be able to tell who his master was. Not surprisingly, we twenty-first-century Christians are called to follow the exact same program that Timothy did.

To "pursue" righteousness—that's a lifelong endeavor that requires our conscious effort and all our energies. Consulting several other English Bible translations of the verb "to pursue" can give us a bigger picture of what God is asking of us: *Fasten attention on* says one. Another talks about *striving after*, and still a third urges us to *aim for* the goals of righteousness, faith, love, and peace. Like a runner pressing toward the finish line or an archer taking aim at the target, we are called to fix our eyes on the goal and concentrate all our efforts on attaining it.

There's also a flip side to this program: In order to attain our goals, we have to avoid the negative forms of conduct that would set us on a different path. To this end, Paul urged Timothy to "shun youthful passions" and "have nothing to do with" pointless controversies and quarrelling (2 Timothy 2:22-23). Again, various English translations amplify Paul's directions: *Avoid* them. *Stay away from* them. *Don't get involved in* them. *Flee or run from* them. *Turn your back on* them. The best way to "cleanse" ourselves so we can become God's "special utensils . . . ready for every good work" is to do our best to avoid sin at all cost (2:21).

The best part about adopting this program is that we will become more and more like Jesus and reflect his glory to others. And that is how we become useful vessels in the hands of the Lord.

Putting both sides of this lifetime program into action—and achieving good results—is not something God expects us to do on our own. As we rely on the power of the Holy Spirit, we will discover godly power that produces amazing results. As St. Jane de Chantal once wrote: "Hold your eyes on God and leave the doing to him. That is all the doing you have to worry about, and the only activity which God asks of you and towards which it is he alone who is drawing you."

"Jesus, I want to fix my eyes on you and pursue that holiness without which no one will see you (Hebrews 12:14). I know that I can only do that with your grace. Help me, Lord, so that I can reflect your love and your perfection."

2 Timothy 3:1-9

^{1} You must understand this, that in the last days distressing times will come. ^{2}For people will be lovers of themselves, lovers of money, boasters, arrogant, abusive, disobedient to their parents, ungrateful, unholy, ^{3}inhuman, implacable, slanderers, profligates, brutes, haters of good, ^{4}treacherous, reckless, swollen with conceit, lovers of pleasure rather than lovers of God, ^{5}holding to the outward form of godliness but denying its power. Avoid them! ^{6}For among them are those who make their way into households and captivate silly women, overwhelmed by their sins and swayed by all kinds of desires, ^{7}who are always being instructed and can never arrive at a knowledge of the truth. ^{8}As Jannes and Jambres opposed Moses, so these people, of corrupt mind and counterfeit faith, also oppose the truth. ^{9}But they will not make much progress, because, as in the case of those two men, their folly will become plain to everyone.

Jewish tradition gave the names Jannes and Jambres to the Egyptian magicians whom Pharaoh called upon to oppose Moses. In their pride and arrogance, they set themselves against God's messenger and even mimicked the miracles worked by Moses and his brother, Aaron. Their tricks, however, were devoid of any real substance, counterfeits only of God's power (Exodus 7:11-12, 20-22; 8:7, 18; 9:11).

Paul warned Timothy that false teachers would be active while the Christians in Ephesus awaited the return of Christ. Like the Egyptian conjurers, such teachers would oppose God and the truth of the gospel with falsehoods and deceptions. While they might seem to "have religion"—"holding the outward form of godliness"—they would deny its power (2 Timothy 3:5). Moreover, with their misleading and false arguments, they would try to win the attention of those who were curious about all sorts of "spiritual" notions and lead the unwary and naïve astray. But, like Jannes and Jambres, these false teachers would ultimately have no real power or substance. Discerning Christians would recognize that their minds were corrupt and their faith counterfeit (3:6-8). Paul was confident that the difference between genuine Christianity and its counterfeits would be clear.

Not many years after Paul wrote these words of warning, St. Ignatius, the bishop of Antioch, wrote similar lines to St. Polycarp, the bishop of Smyrna and a fellow disciple of the apostle John: "Do not let yourself be upset by those who seem to be very reliable and yet put forward strange teachings. Stand your guard like an anvil under the hammer" (*To Polycarp*, 3).

Things haven't changed much since the early days of the church. We still need to be on guard against those who distort the gospel message, promote "wisdom" promising heightened consciousness and supernatural experiences, and suggest immoral conduct. Just as in Paul's time, we too need to discern what is in accord with Christ and his truth and reject what is contrary to the purity of the gospel. St. Ignatius' advice in another letter is still to the point: "Keep away from strange fare, by which I mean heresy. For those people mix Jesus Christ with their teachings, speaking things unworthy of belief. It is as if they were giving a deadly poison mixed with sweetened wine, so that the unsuspecting victim readily accepts it and drinks his own death with fatal pleasure" (*To the Trallians*, 6).

God wants to give all of us gifts of discernment, prudence, and good judgment, just as he has showered them upon his church. All he asks is that we take steps of faith in exercising these gifts.

"Come, Holy Spirit, and give me confidence in your work in my heart. By your power, open my eyes to see and my ears to hear, so that I may discern truth from deception, and light from darkness."

2 Timothy 3:10-15

[10] Now you have observed my teaching, my conduct, my aim in life, my faith, my patience, my love, my steadfastness, [11]my persecutions, and my suffering the things that happened to me in Antioch, Iconium, and Lystra. What persecutions I endured! Yet the Lord rescued me from all of them. [12]Indeed, all who want to live a godly life in Christ Jesus will be persecuted. [13]But wicked people and impostors will go from bad to worse, deceiving others and being deceived. [14]But as for you, continue in what you have learned and firmly believed, knowing from whom you learned it, [15]and how from childhood you have known the sacred writings that are able to instruct you for salvation through faith in Christ Jesus.

Very often it is those closest to us during our childhood who have the greatest effect on our lives. We tend to remember our first girlfriend or boyfriend, or our "best friend" from the neighborhood. Each of us probably can point to one (or maybe more) of our high school teachers who opened our eyes to the wider world and inspired us to want to learn.

This seems to be the case with Timothy. His mother, Eunice, and his grandmother, Lois, played a major part in his formation, especially in their ability to pass on faith in Christ and a passionate adherence to the gospel (2 Timothy 1:5). They must have been powerful influences indeed, considering that Timothy's father was a pagan (Acts 16:1). In a patriarchal society such as Timothy's, it was typically the father who set the tone and direction for a child's formation. It must have taken two very forceful personalities to be able to redirect the young man in so fundamental a way.

Parents have an awesome privilege—and responsibility—to be models of faith within their families, especially when the parents themselves are divided in their convictions. Paul addressed just such a situation when he wrote to the believers in Corinth, "The unbelieving husband is made holy through his wife, and the unbelieving wife is made holy through her husband. . . . Wife, for all you know, you might save your husband. Husband, for all you know, you might save your wife" (1 Corinthians 7:14,16). Addressing a similar situation, St. Peter wrote: "Wives . . . accept the authority of your husbands, so that, even if some of them do not obey the word, they may be won over without a word by their wives' conduct, when they see the purity and reverence of your lives" (1 Peter 3:1-2).

Is it possible that this was the strategy employed by Eunice and Lois? We can imagine them, rather than forcing an issue or causing deep divisions in their family, manifesting the love and peace of Christ in their home to such a degree that the young Timothy was won over and began to pay attention to the stories they told about Abraham, Moses, David, and ultimately, Jesus himself (2 Timothy 3:15).

According to the *Catechism of the Catholic Church*, "A wholesome family life can foster interior dispositions that are a genuine preparation for a living faith and remain a support for it throughout one's life" (2225). This appears to be the principle by which Eunice and Lois worked, and it is a principle that can guide us today as well. May we all strive to manifest Jesus to everyone around us—especially our children and grandchildren! They are always observing us, and our influence upon them can be great indeed!

"Jesus, make me so much like you that when my family sees me, they see your light shining clear and bright. Lord, bring every member of my family to deep faith and trust in you."

2 Timothy 3:16-17

[16]All scripture is inspired by God and is useful for teaching, for reproof, for correction, and for training in righteousness, [17]so that everyone who belongs to God may be proficient, equipped for every good work.

In the long years before Jesus was born, God revealed himself through supernatural manifestations of his presence. We need only think about his presence in the burning bush and his parting of the Red Sea during the time of the Exodus, or the dramatic way he spoke to prophets like Ezekiel and Isaiah during the time of the kings. These revelations—along with the revelation of the law and the godly wisdom manifest in the psalms and proverbs—is contained in the books of the Hebrew Bible. These are the Scriptures that Timothy was taught by his mother Eunice, and they are the same Scriptures that Paul urged Timothy to hold fast to.

The fact that Paul called the Scriptures "inspired by God" (or "God-breathed") reveals an understanding that the Bible is far more than a list of dos and don'ts, or a collection of lofty ideals and noble characters for our imitation. Paul clearly knew that Scripture contains many moral lessons and uplifting stories, but he also knew that there was something that set it apart from any other book ever written. He knew that Scripture is *the mind and heart of God revealed to man*. In a sense, just as Jesus is the Word of God in human form, Scripture is the grace of God in written form. In other words, as powerful and life changing as Jesus is, *that* is how powerful and life-changing Scripture can be for us.

To experience the power of Scripture, we simply need to accept that our thoughts are not God's thoughts. Are you open to seeing things differently? Are you willing to let God change your mindset? If so, then you're ready to let Scripture *pierce* your heart and *form* your mind.

Of course, while God does the work, you will still have to be attentive and available to God as you read. Through his parable of the sower and the seed, Jesus illustrated the ability of his word to bear fruit when it falls on good soil. So start today. Soak your mind in God's word. Dwell on the readings you hear at Mass. Let every quiet time with Scripture become a time of intimate conversation with the Lord. Scripture reading is so much more than an intellectual inquiry.

As you open your mind to his words and allow the truths he speaks to be written on your heart—as his word becomes "flesh" in you—you will be transformed into God's own image. So believe that his word always accomplishes what he intends. And his intention is to unite you with him forever.

"Holy Spirit, open my heart to the power of Scripture. Help me to learn God's ways. Make me into good soil that receives your precious words and bears the fruit of your love."

2 Timothy 4:1-8

[1] In the presence of God and of Christ Jesus, who is to judge the living and the dead, and in view of his appearing and his kingdom, I solemnly urge you: [2]proclaim the message; be persistent whether the time is favorable or unfavorable; convince, rebuke, and encourage, with the utmost patience in teaching. [3]For the time is coming when people will not put up with sound doctrine, but having itching ears, they will accumulate for themselves teachers to suit their own desires, [4]and will turn away from listening to the truth and

wander away to myths. [5]As for you, always be sober, endure suffering, do the work of an evangelist, carry out your ministry fully.
[6] As for me, I am already being poured out as a libation, and the time of my departure has come. [7]I have fought the good fight, I have finished the race, I have kept the faith. [8]From now on there is reserved for me the crown of righteousness, which the Lord, the righteous judge, will give me on that day, and not only to me but also to all who have longed for his appearing.

How applicable are these words to us today! The message of this centuries-old letter could very easily be part of any pastoral letter to our parishes. Many of the issues it addresses are ones we also face as we try to live out the gospel message. Though this letter is addressed to the pastor of a first-century church, it could have been just as easily written to all of us, for we are all members of a "royal priesthood, a holy nation, God's own people" (1 Peter 2:9).

In the letter, Timothy is reminded of his commission to preach the word of God with urgency and steadfastness. Not only was he to be an evangelist and a teacher; he was also called to be a guardian of his followers—an important, and at times unpleasant, task. As any pastor today knows, leading a "flock" sometimes means dealing with accusations, false teachings, and deviations from the true message given by Jesus. Then, as today, many were preoccupied with myths and speculations, interpreting the gospel to suit their whims.

Today, many seek to justify sin. We still have great disregard for life as we kill the unborn and the aged, and as we chase after false gods such as material wealth and worldly status. So many "philosophies" directly contradict the gospel message—ideas and "alternatives" leading God's children away form truth and light. Like Timothy, God calls us to remain steadfast in our faith. We may find ourselves drifting into the confusion of popular concepts and values. Who can save us? Who can comfort us? Who can lead us into the truth? Only Jesus.

Let us seek Jesus' presence and abide in his word today. He will guide us to clarity. Jesus promised that the Holy Spirit would be with us to teach us and comfort us. As we spend time with Scripture and allow the Spirit to speak to our hearts and minds, he will lead us to deeper conversion and a fuller embrace of the truth. As we spend time every day in prayer, we become formed into a people after the Lord's own heart.

"Heavenly Father, help us to run the race and fight the good fight of faith. We believe that you are present to us and will continue to protect and bless us as your church, a people set apart for your glory and honor."

2 Timothy 4:10-17

[10][F]or Demas, in love with this present world, has deserted me and gone to Thessalonica; Crescens has gone to Galatia, Titus to Dalmatia. [11]Only Luke is with me. Get Mark and bring him with you, for he is useful in my ministry. [12]I have sent Tychicus to Ephesus. [13]When you come, bring the cloak that I left with Carpus at Troas, also the books, and above all the parchments. [14]Alexander the coppersmith did me great harm; the Lord will pay him back for his deeds. [15]You also must beware of him, for he strongly opposed our message.

[16] At my first defense no one came to my support, but all deserted me. May it not be counted against them! [17]But the Lord stood by me and gave me strength, so that through me the message might be

fully proclaimed and all the Gentiles might hear it. So I was rescued from the lion's mouth. ✏

L uke is well known as the "beloved physician" (Colossians 4:14) and the careful compiler of the third gospel and the Acts of the Apostles. Less well known, however, is his gift for steadfast friendship. Luke stood by Paul in good times and bad, for better and for worse, for richer and for poorer, in sickness and in health—almost as if he had taken a marriage vow! When Paul was put under house arrest in Rome, Luke alone remained with him (2 Timothy 4:11). And even when death parted the two friends, the separation was only temporary: They now live reunited before God's throne.

As one of Paul's fellow workers, Luke shared his labors and faced many of the perils that he encountered: imprisonments, beatings, shipwrecks, sleepless nights, hunger, thirst, cold, dangers from traitors and bandits (2 Corinthians 11:23-27). Paul endured them all, and Luke was right there with him. Together they loved Jesus, and together they lived out the heart of the gospel: "No one has greater love than this, to lay down one's life for one's friends" (John 15:13).

The ideal of friendship that St. Luke demonstrated should open our eyes to the steadfast love God wants to give us for each other. He is always ready to pour out special blessings when we put aside our inclinations to be friendly only when it's easy or convenient. God loves it when we stand by each other through thick or thin, for the sake of the gospel.

Despite all the hardships involved, don't overlook the fact that real Christian friendship has some fabulous consolations. Never doubt for a moment that Paul and Luke had great times together. As they traveled to spread the gospel throughout their world, they received warm hospitality at times and celebrated the love of God. They had opportunities to rejoice at extraordinary miracles and healings and to marvel at the ways God rescued them. They experienced the grateful love of thousands who were converted by their message—multitudes, when you add in all the people like ourselves, who still benefit from their work and still love these men today!

"Thank you, Lord, for St. Luke's example of friendship and service. Thank you for the friends you give us. Help us to be good friends, even to the point of laying down our lives."

2 Timothy 4:19-22

[19] Greet Prisca and Aquila, and the household of Onesiphorus. [20]Erastus remained in Corinth; Trophimus I left ill in Miletus. [21]Do your best to come before winter. Eubulus sends greetings to you, as do Pudens and Linus and Claudia and all the brothers and sisters. [22] The Lord be with your spirit. Grace be with you.

The warm exchange of greetings with which Paul concluded this letter to Timothy—and the personal greetings included in each letter of his in the New Testament—reveal how deeply he valued and loved his co-workers. They were not just fellow apostles and disciples who shared in his zeal and in his labors for the Lord. They were *friends* who had a place in his heart.

Prisca and Aquila . . . Erastus . . . Trophimus . . . Eubulus . . . Pudens . . . Linus . . . Claudia. Each of these men and women had been touched by the gospel message as it spread through the Mediterranean world. They loved Jesus deeply, and their lives had been transformed by the power of his Spirit. Prisca and Aquila were, like Paul, tentmakers as well as missionary evangelists (Acts 18:2-3, 18, 26; 1 Corinthians 16:19). They had even risked their lives for Paul (Romans 16:3-4). According to tradition, Pudens was a Roman senator converted by Peter. Many scholars identify Linus as one of Rome's earliest bishops and as successor of Peter, the second pope; Claudia is thought to have been Linus' mother.

Although very little is known about the lives of these people, their names have been revered by Christians through the ages because of Paul's love for them and because of their witness as members of the early church. We should be deeply grateful for these first-century believers since they are our forebears in the faith. They—and their contributions to the life and growth of their communities in Asia Minor and in Rome—are the foundation stones of the worldwide church we belong to today.

Just as it was in the first century, the church of the twenty-first century is a living network of personal relationships. Knit together in love as brothers and sisters in the Lord, we have the privilege of serving side by side for the sake of the gospel. Our fellow parishioners who serve in the music ministry or take Communion to the sick, staff workers at the local Christian counseling center, missionary sisters caring for abandoned children in India—these are the contemporary Timothys and Priscas and Aquilas who make up the living church today. Let's pray for one another as each of us contributes to the upbuilding of the body of Christ.

"Thank you, Father, for all my brothers and sisters in Christ. Unite us together in love as we serve you and your church."

To My Faithful Brother and Co-worker . . .

The Letter to Titus

To My Faithful Brother and Co-worker

To My Faithful Brother and Co-worker . . .

An Introduction to the Letter to Titus

by Fr. Joseph F. Wimmer, OSA

In his Second Letter to the Corinthians, Paul mentions his friend and protégé Titus at least nine times. He calls him his "brother" (2 Corinthians 2:13), who brought him consolation and joy (7:6, 13); and his "partner" whose virtues Paul deeply appreciated (8:23; 7:14) and whom he sent as a missionary to guide the people of Corinth about certain matters (12:18). In the Letter to the Galatians, Paul refers to Titus again, this time as a traveling companion on the way to Jerusalem (Galatians 2:1), and explains that though Titus was of Greek origin, he had not been compelled to be circumcised after his conversion to Christianity, even though some Jewish Christians thought that he should have been.

According to 2 Timothy 4:10, Paul had sent Titus as a missionary to Dalmatia (modern Yugoslavia), but he ended up as the head of the Christian community on the island of Crete (Titus 1:4-5), where Paul himself had preached (Acts 27:7-12).

The inhabitants of Crete in Paul's time were a combination of Greeks, Romans, and Jews. The Greeks, known as the Dorians, had an ancient militaristic culture, much like that of ancient Sparta. They were defeated, however, by the Romans in 87 B.C. and became part of the Roman Empire. The presence of Jews on the island is attested to by Philo's *Embassy to Gaius*. Crete became an important Roman province because it defended the sea routes between Rome and Egypt and

Syria. It enjoyed peace for many centuries, until it was captured by Arabs from Spain in A.D. 826.

Date and Manner of Pauline Authorship. Since the early 1800s, scholars have debated whether or not St. Paul was actually the author of the Letter to Titus. Although the letter claims to have been written by Paul, some scholars point out that it lacks many of the words Paul regularly used, such as "body," "cross," "freedom," and "covenant," and that it contains Greek words or expressions found nowhere else in Paul's clearly authentic letters, such as "piety," "epiphany," "good conscience," and "trustworthy word." There is also mention of deacons and *episcopoi* ("overseers" or "bishops"), which seems to point to a later development of the early church, perhaps as late as A.D. 100. If this is so, then it is likely that this letter comes from a disciple of St. Paul, following an ancient custom of writing in the spirit of a great predecessor at some time after his death.

Ultimately it makes little difference whether the Letter to Titus was written by Paul himself or by a later disciple. No matter who put pen to parchment, this letter clearly represents Paul's thought, as well as the beliefs of the early Christian community. Moreover, the Letter to Titus has been accepted almost universally as the word of God, inspired by the Holy Spirit working through a human author. So whoever wrote Titus, Christians everywhere read it now not only out of historical interest, to find out what happened in the ancient past, but primarily with faith in God as a guide for our lives today.

In a mere forty-six verses, this letter tackles the basic issues behind a correct understanding of the gospel: salvation by God's grace accepted in faith and by baptism into the church; the body of Christ as the living community and the new people of God founded on the twelve apostles; and the role and necessity of authority within the community of the church. These issues—and especially the last one—have always existed and were particularly acute as the first century closed and the second century began. Hence, various aspects of authority and obedience loom large in this letter and remain relevant, even though the precise concerns may be different.

An Outline. After the greeting from Paul to Titus, there follows a brief description of the virtues of the spiritual leaders of the community. These leaders are to be especially cautious about certain false teachings and practices taught by "those of the circumcision," possibly Christians who had formerly been Jews, or, as will be explained later, a group who used Jewish genealogies to form a secret teaching akin to Gnosticism. Chapter 2 lists the duties of Christians in the home, and in Chapter 3, Christian responsibilities toward the larger society are discussed. The letter then concludes with a short exhortation and blessing.

Greeting (1:1-4). Paul, a "servant of God and apostle of Jesus Christ," is called to strengthen the faith of "God's chosen ones" in the "hope of eternal life." It was Paul who first used the expression "faith, hope, and charity" in the New Testament; and here we find faith and hope mentioned together again. The reality of eternal life that forms the basis of Christian hope was promised by God "before time began," so it is a most firm basis on which to build our lives.

Presbyters and **Episkopoi** *(1:5-9).* Titus is asked to appoint presbyters in every town of Crete. The Greek term *presbyteros*, from which we get the English word "priest," is a translation of the Hebrew for "elder," and refers to a group of religious leaders in the local community. According to 1 Timothy 4:14, presbyters were installed by the imposition of hands, much like the transfer of authority from Moses to

Joshua in Numbers 27:18-23 or the official appointment of the seven deacons in Acts 6:6 and of Paul and Barnabas as missionaries in Acts 13:3. Since they would be singled out as role models in the community, presbyters were expected to be married only once and to have raised children in the faith.

Verses 7 to 9 describe the necessary qualities of the *episkopos*, the "steward of God." Apparently the *episkopos*, a Greek title from which the English noun "bishop" and adjective "episcopal" derives, was the head of the group of elders. In secular Greek and Hebrew, the title was that of an overseer. The concept of bishops today, as successors of the apostles and as the only ones who could ordain men to the priesthood, comes from a slightly later development of church ministry during the middle of the second century. At Crete, and in many parts of the first-century church, religious authority resided in the groups of presbyters or elders, with one of their own as *episkopos* or overseer at their head. The *episkopos*, or "bishop," was to be hospitable, temperate, holy, firmly rooted in the faith, and able to refute opponents.

False Teachers (1:10-16). The false teachers "of the circumcision" are excoriated by furious invective as rebellious "idle talkers and deceivers," but the precise nature of their errors is never clearly given. Titus 1:14 mentions Jewish myths and "commandments of those who reject the truth," and 3:9 urges Titus to "avoid stupid controversies, genealogies, dissensions, and quarrels about the law." If 1 Timothy 6:20 is a parallel warning to "avoid the profane chatter and contradictions of what is falsely called knowledge," then both texts may be addressing the same basic problem, the beginnings of Gnosticism, against which the Fathers of the Church fought with such vehemence.

Gnosticism was a system of belief that posited intermediary forces between the soul and God, and focused on the soul's passage through the seven spheres on the way to heaven—a passage that could only be accomplished by secret *gnosis*, or "knowledge." The Gnostics claimed to have that knowledge, which may well be referred to as Jewish myths and genealogies (Titus 1:14 and 3:9). Entire Gnostic systems were built on lists of intermediaries between God and the world, using material from the Bible and extra-biblical literature, along with their own speculations. "They profess to know God, but they deny him by their actions" (Titus 1:16).

Duties of Christians in the Home (2:1-10). After denouncing false teachers, Paul lists some of the ways in which Christians are to conduct themselves properly, both at home and in the larger society. Advice is given first to older men and women, then to younger women and men, and finally to slaves. The older men are to be temperate and to practice the virtues of faith, love, and perseverance. This list of virtues is reminiscent of Paul's call for faith, hope, and love in 1 Corinthians 13:13. Older women are not to gossip or become intoxicated, but should teach younger women to love their families and be faithful. Young men must learn to control themselves as well.

Telling "slaves to be submissive to their masters" (Titus 2:9) may strike us as harsh, but Paul and the early Christians knew that they could neither ignore the Roman system of slavery nor directly fight it. They could, however, insist that all human beings, men and women, slaves and free, are "one" in Christ Jesus (Galatians 3:28). The radical call to mutual love that was at the heart of early Christianity set into motion social changes so strong that eventually slavery came to be seen as intrinsically wrong and something that needed to be abolished.

Transformation of Life (2:11-15). As we wait for the second coming of Jesus, the one who sacrificed himself for us, we can trust that the grace of God will guide us to act with prudence, justice, fortitude, and temperance—the cardinal virtues listed in Wisdom 8:7. They are called "cardinal" because all the other virtues hinge on them, and the word for "hinge" is *cardo*. By focusing on these fundamental virtues, Paul of course expects us to put into practice many others, according to whatever is appropriate in different situations.

Civic Responsibilities (3:1-8). Paul urges loyalty to government officials, courtesy to everyone, and not speaking evil of others. He explains that "we"—himself included—were once disobedient and slaves to passion, but have now been saved by the mercy of God through baptism and the gift of the Holy Spirit. Because we are now heirs to eternal life, we are filled with hope!

Final Directives (3:9-11). Several times in this letter, Paul stresses the importance of doing good works (Titus 2:14; 3:8), that is, leading a good life, something that was made possible by God's prior saving action. Titus is thus called to refrain from arguing with troublemakers about genealogies or other useless matters. Instead, after warning false teachers twice, he is not to have anything more to do with them. They have gone astray and condemn themselves, even as Titus and his people continue to follow the good works to which they have been called.

Farewell Greetings (3:12-15). At the end of this letter, we learn that Artemas and Tychicus—two other coworkers of Paul's—were going to take Titus' place at Crete so that Titus could join Paul at Nicopolis (probably in western Greece). Zenas the lawyer and Apollo were also leaving Crete, and Titus was asked to see to it that they were well provided for. Then, one last time, Paul exhorted the community to "good works," this time in working hard so that they could provide for these travelers. The focus—as always—is on charity. And what better way to make ourselves "fruitful" than in pouring out our lives in service to others? And on this note, Paul's companions send greetings, while Paul himself ends with a blessing that has become a standard part of our prayer together as believers: "May grace be with you all!"

To My Faithful Brother and Co-worker

Titus 1:1-9

¹ Paul, a servant of God and an apostle of Jesus Christ, for the sake of the faith of God's elect and the knowledge of the truth that is in accordance with godliness, ²in the hope of eternal life that God, who never lies, promised before the ages began—³in due time he revealed his word through the proclamation with which I have been entrusted by the command of God our Savior,

⁴ To Titus, my loyal child in the faith we share:

Grace and peace from God the Father and Christ Jesus our Savior.

⁵ I left you behind in Crete for this reason, so that you should put in order what remained to be done, and should appoint elders in every town, as I directed you: ⁶someone who is blameless, married only once, whose children are believers, not accused of debauchery and not rebellious. ⁷For a bishop, as God's steward, must be blameless; he must not be arrogant or quick-tempered or addicted to wine or violent or greedy for gain; ⁸but he must be hospitable, a lover of goodness, prudent, upright, devout, and self-controlled. ⁹He must have a firm grasp of the word that is trustworthy in accordance with the teaching, so that he may be able both to preach with sound doctrine and to refute those who contradict it.

The Letter to Titus, along with the First and Second Letters to Timothy, comprise what are known as the pastoral epistles of the New Testament. These letters reflect a concern in the early church for congregational matters and attest to the conviction that St. Paul's teaching was indeed inspired. Many biblical scholars question whether the Letter to Titus was actually written by Paul, yet they do recognize that the letter contains statements that are consistent with Paul's teaching and that it functioned as a guide for the primitive church.

The pastoral epistles reveal a concern in the church that apt teachers be appointed who could combat the threat of heresy. As the older leaders who had been commissioned by Christ and the apostles began to die, and as the church spread and grew, it became essential to guarantee the orthodoxy and reliability of church leaders.

The appointment of "elders" spoken of in Titus mirrors the Old Testament tradition in which Moses named trustworthy leaders to help him care for the Israelites (Numbers 11:16-17, 24-25). In New Testament times, each Jewish community had its own council of elders similar to the Sanhedrin. Conforming to this structure, Paul and Barnabas appointed elders in the churches they established on their missionary journeys (Acts 14:23). For the apostles, it was vital that the new leaders demonstrate irreproachable character and unquestionable faithfulness to apostolic teaching. These elders—the apostles' successors—are the spiritual ancestors of the church's bishops today.

The Fathers of the Second Vatican Council taught that bishops—successors of the apostles and shepherds of the church—have a very high calling: "[The holders of office], who are endowed with sacred power, serve their brethren, so that all . . . may arrive at salvation" (Dogmatic Constitution on the Church, 18). This calling, like that described in the Letter to Titus, places first priority on preaching and teaching: "For bishops are preachers of the faith, who lead new disciples to Christ, and they are authentic teachers. . . . By the light of the Holy Spirit [they] illustrate that faith" (25).

Let us pray today for all our bishops throughout the world: "Lord, you have called our leaders to serve us in preaching the gospel. Protect them from all harm and error, and by the power of your Spirit enable them to demonstrate to the world the power of your resurrection and the majesty of your love."

Titus 1:10-16

[10] There are also many rebellious people, idle talkers and deceivers, especially those of the circumcision; [11]they must be silenced, since they are upsetting whole families by teaching for sordid gain what it is not right to teach. [12]It was one of them, their very own prophet, who said,

"Cretans are always liars, vicious brutes, lazy gluttons."

[13] That testimony is true. For this reason rebuke them sharply, so that they may become sound in the faith, [14]not paying attention to Jewish myths or to commandments of those who reject the truth. [15]To the pure all things are pure, but to the corrupt and unbelieving nothing is pure. Their very minds and consciences are corrupted. [16]They profess to know God, but they deny him by their actions. They are detestable, disobedient, unfit for any good work.

Part of our obligation as followers of Jesus is to know the truths of the gospel so that we can live it with our whole hearts and pass it on to the next generation. But living as a Christian also involves protecting the faith we profess from the influences of false or spurious teachings. In some cases, it may even entail publicly refuting these false teachings in order to protect the welfare of the Christian community. This passage from Titus highlights such a situation.

From its earliest days, Christianity faced the challenge posed by Jewish believers who insisted that Christians had to become Jews first and follow Jewish laws. In these verses from Titus, it appears that the challenge had become a serious problem for Titus and for the believers in Crete who were under his leadership. What began as a genuine concern and reverence for the Law of Moses had degenerated into a point of contention as Jewish dietary laws were being forced upon believers from gentile backgrounds (Titus 1:14-15).

Paul consistently taught the good news that believers in Christ were not obligated to complete their salvation by embracing conformity to Jewish laws. He felt so passionately about the absolutely free gift of salvation that he called those who taught that conformity *was* necessary, "liars." Since the citizens of Crete had a reputation throughout the Roman Empire for being liars, Paul's charge against these false teachers in Crete had particular force and meaning.

Our faith is based upon the truths of the word of God and the preaching and teaching that have come down to us from the apostles themselves. Whenever murky or false teaching is mixed in with these truths, there is a real threat that our faith will be weakened. That's why it is vital that we guard our minds and hearts and submit everything we hear to the Scriptures and the teachings of the church. Two ways that we can do this are to study the Scriptures directly and to get to know the *Catechism of the Catholic Church*. Don't be afraid to take these steps! Don't let the task intimidate or daunt you! The Holy Spirit is the best teacher in the world, and he is ready right now to fill you with his truths, his wisdom, and his grace.

"Blessed Holy Spirit, Jesus promised that you would lead us into all truth. Help me to grow in and guard my faith so that I can share it with those around me."

Titus 2:1-10

[1]   But as for you, teach what is consistent with sound doctrine. [2]Tell the older men to be temperate, serious, prudent, and sound in faith, in love, and in endurance.
[3]   Likewise, tell the older women to be reverent in behavior, not to be slanderers or slaves to drink; they are to teach what is good, [4]so that they may encourage the young women to love their husbands, to love their children, [5]to be self-controlled, chaste, good managers of the household, kind, being submissive to their husbands, so that the word of God may not be discredited.
[6]   Likewise, urge the younger men to be self-controlled. [7]Show yourself in all respects a model of good works, and in your teaching show integrity, gravity, [8]and sound speech that cannot be censured; then any opponent will be put to shame, having nothing evil to say of us.
[9]   Tell slaves to be submissive to their masters and to give satisfaction in every respect; they are not to talk back, [10]not to pilfer, but to show complete and perfect fidelity, so that in everything they may be an ornament to the doctrine of God our Savior.

J*ust say no*. This slogan has been used in many programs trying to help young people avoid drug abuse. Notwithstanding the good intentions and hard work of those involved in these programs, however, many people, young and old, do not have the power to say no. It is obvious that it takes more than clever slogans and good intentions—even more than heroic dedication—to change the drives and behavior of a fallen humanity.

The letter to Titus shows us what is necessary if we want to grow in personal holiness and help others lead godly lives. First, we need to have our minds formed by "sound doctrine" (Titus 2:1), which comes from Scripture and the teaching of the church. Second, we need to follow the example of godly men and women, whose lives show that it is possible to live out the gospel message faithfully (2:6-8). Finally, and most importantly, we need to trust in God's unending grace, which teaches us "to renounce impiety and worldly passions, and in the present age to live lives that are self controlled, upright, and godly " (2:11-12).

The *Catechism of the Catholic Church* defines grace as "the free and undeserved help that God gives us to respond to his call" (1996). "Grace is a participation in the life of God. It introduces us into the intimacy of Trinitarian life" (1997). It is "the gratuitous gift that God makes to us of his own life, infused by the Holy Spirit into our soul to heal it of sin and to sanctify it" (1999).

As we seek to live as children of God and witnesses to the gospel, let us remember all that is ours in Christ. God has generously given us everything we need to reflect his glory and to live in hopeful expectation of the day when Jesus returns to bring us into the fullness of his life. Let us turn our hearts to Jesus, who "gave himself for us that he might redeem us from all iniquity and purify for himself a people of his own who are zealous for good deeds" (Titus 2:14). Through baptism into his life, we have received grace in abundance. Let us open our hearts to this life-changing grace and respond to it in confident faith.

"Father, you are the author of amazing, unending, all-powerful grace. Teach me how to be as generous in receiving this grace as you are in pouring it out!"

Titus 2:11-15

[11] For the grace of God has appeared, bringing salvation to all, [12]training us to renounce impiety and worldly passions, and in the present age to live lives that are self-controlled, upright, and godly, [13]while we wait for the blessed hope and the manifestation of the glory of our great God and Savior, Jesus Christ. [14]He it is who gave himself for us that he might redeem us from all iniquity and purify for himself a people of his own who are zealous for good deeds. [15] Declare these things; exhort and reprove with all authority. Let no one look down on you.

The grace of God has appeared . . . training us. . . . —*Titus 2:11, 12*

Have you ever stopped to consider the radical nature of this claim? God doesn't pour out his grace just to help us out of tough scrapes or to comfort us when we fall. He gives grace to *train* us: to form us and to educate us. Let's take a look at some of the ways that God does this for us.

Paul writes that God has given us his grace to train us "to *reject godless ways* and worldly desires." It's one of the Holy Spirit's most important jobs to help us to identify those dimensions in our lives that are worldly and separated from the godliness to which we are called. Then once we have identified them, we have nothing less than godly grace to help us reject sin and change our hearts. At the same time, as we learn to be open to godly grace, we will begin to *desire* and *pursue* those things that are at the heart of the kingdom of God: purity, simplicity, honesty, and fellowship.

God's grace also trains us how to *live*. God has given us his Spirit to teach us the temperance, justice, and devotion that work together to form us in the image of Christ. Through trial and error, through prayer and Scripture, we come to learn how to use the things of this world without becoming ensnared by them. We learn how to recognize just and unjust situations and conditions, and a desire grows in us to work for justice, both in our homes and in the world around us.

Sometimes we think that we have to do all of the study and training and education—whether for ourselves or for the sake of our children. But God doesn't want us to do anything alone or in a vacuum. He is always there, ready to teach us and to form us. He is in every situation, ready to lead us and guide us. So try yielding to the grace of God in you. Let his Spirit inspire you in the way that you should go. There's nothing like entering the "school of Christ" and having none other than the Holy Spirit as your personal tutor!

"Dear Lord, send your grace more fully into my life to train me and mold me for holiness and righteousness. Help me to yield more and more to your work in my life."

Titus 3:1-7

[1] Remind them to be subject to rulers and authorities, to be obedient, to be ready for every good work, [2]to speak evil of no one, to avoid quarreling, to be gentle, and to show every courtesy to everyone. [3]For we ourselves were once foolish, disobedient, led astray, slaves to various passions and pleasures, passing our days in malice and envy, despicable, hating one another. [4]But when the goodness and loving kindness of God our Savior appeared, [5]he saved us, not because of any works of righteousness that we had

done, but according to his mercy, through the water of rebirth and renewal by the Holy Spirit. [6]This Spirit he poured out on us richly through Jesus Christ our Savior, [7]so that, having been justified by his grace, we might become heirs according to the hope of eternal life. ✍

G od is aware of everything that is hidden in our hearts, even the sin which can so easily enslave us. He knows that sin consists not only in outward actions, but also in the thoughts and attitudes of the heart; he knows that because of sin, we were cut off from his loving plan for us. But God so desired to fill us with the power to follow him, that through Jesus, he has provided a way for us to be healed and to receive a whole new life.

As he preached about this passage from Titus, St. John Chrysostom (c. 347–407) emphasized the fact that we need much more than purification from sin—we need a whole new birth. He compared fallen man to a house in a state of ruin, saying that for such a house, "No one places props under it, or makes any addition to the old building, but pulls it down to its foundations and rebuilds it anew" (On Titus, Homily 5).

This is the reality of what began at our baptism. We were made into a completely new creation by water and the Spirit. Baptism is not merely a "dusting off" of our old lives. If that is all we needed, surely the Father would not have sent Jesus to give his life for us. No, we were brought to a rebirth in which everything was made new!

In his unending generosity, God did not stop with our baptism. He knew that our new life would need constant nurturing. This is why he pours his Spirit upon us in such abundance (Titus 3:6). God doesn't just give us the Spirit to strengthen us; he gives us the Spirit so that his work in us may be brought to completion and perfection.

Every day, the Spirit finds opportunities to teach us to think with God, to show us the Father's love, and to put a longing for Jesus into our hearts. Every day, the Spirit wants to fill us with the joy and expectancy of what the Father can do in and through us as we follow him.

"Lord, giver of new life, you have truly loved us and provided everything we need to be restored to you. We look to you for the Spirit who is able to deepen your life within us. Thank you, Father, for your perfect plan to make us heirs with Jesus!"

Titus 3:8-11

8   The saying is sure.

I desire that you insist on these things, so that those who have come to believe in God may be careful to devote themselves to good works; these things are excellent and profitable to everyone. 9But avoid stupid controversies, genealogies, dissensions, and quarrels about the law, for they are unprofitable and worthless. 10After a first and second admonition, have nothing more to do with anyone who causes divisions, 11since you know that such a person is perverted and sinful, being self-condemned.

For all the debate the church has seen on the relationship between faith and works, Scripture makes one thing clear: Good works play a vital role in the Christian life. While faith in Jesus is our primary means of salvation, good works are the concrete evidence that our faith is being expressed in love. In fact, these words from St. Paul encourage us to *devote* ourselves to good works, not just to keep them on the periphery of our lives. Let's explore this call a little more fully.

The *Catechism of the Catholic Church* (2447) identifies some of the more central acts of mercy and love that we are called to embrace:

> Instructing, advising, consoling, and comforting are spiritual works of mercy, as are forgiving and bearing wrongs patiently. The corporal works of mercy consist especially in feeding the hungry, sheltering the homeless, clothing the naked, visiting the sick and imprisoned, and burying the dead.

Obviously, we can't undertake all of these acts ourselves, and we shouldn't just choose which ones we will pursue on a random basis. The best thing we can do is to come before the Lord in prayer and ask him to lead us to those works that he wants us to do. Each of us has been created for a specific set of "good works" (Ephesians 2:10) that God has in store for us. So it stands to reason that as we approach the question of works and service in prayer, we will find ourselves guided to those acts of mercy that will not only build up the kingdom of God but help us keep our eyes and hearts fixed on Jesus as well.

Let us also remember that these "good works" are meant for those who are closest to us as well as for "the needy" outside our circles of influence. It's tempting to think that good works only apply to people we don't really know. But the practical reality is that we have an abundance of opportunities to practice charity and mercy right in our own homes.

So sit down with a piece of paper and a pen and write out the kinds of service to which you feel drawn. Then, pray and ask the Spirit to help guide you as you decide how you can best be an ambassador for Christ in this world. There's no telling how powerful the results can be!

"Lord Jesus, help me identify and eagerly pursue those good works that you have set apart for me to accomplish. Lord, I want to work for your kingdom to come!"

Titus 3:12-15

[12] When I send Artemas to you, or Tychicus, do your best to come to me at Nicopolis, for I have decided to spend the winter there. [13]Make every effort to send Zenas the lawyer and Apollos on their way, and see that they lack nothing. [14]And let people learn to devote themselves to good works in order to meet urgent needs, so that they may not be unproductive.
[15] All who are with me send greetings to you. Greet those who love us in the faith. Grace be with all of you.

In his journey and ministry, Paul was accompanied and aided by many men and women, including Titus and the four he mentions at the close of this letter: Artemus, Tychicus, Zenas, and Apollo. Paul knew the importance of friendship as well as the importance of working with other Christians to spread the teachings of Christ.

Paul was well known for identifying the church as the "body of Christ" (Romans 12; 1 Corinthians 12; Ephesians 4, 5; Colossians 1). He knew by experience that the church, like the human body, consists of many members, all of which are needed, and yet not all have the same function or purpose. He met and worked with many Christian men and women throughout his apostolic ministry, and he formed many close relationships. In the process, his own ministry was strengthened and multiplied, and the efforts of the many had more effect. Paul was hardly a "lone ranger"!

How are your relationships with other Christians? Are you working with others to share in the work of Jesus Christ? Have you joined with others lately in a collaborative effort to strengthen your parish or other church ministry?

Many of us can be hesitant to form these kinds of friendships. We may not feel that we have enough gifts, abilities, and talents to contribute. We may not want to risk the possibility of failure and rejection. Perhaps some past involvement ended badly and left a bad taste in our mouths. The fact remains, though, that each of us plays a vital role in the body of Christ! God has infinite resources, and he always stands ready to show us our gifts and the ways we can use them to serve his people.

If you are working with other Christians in ministry at the present time, keep it up! If you're not, or if your involvement is limited, ask God to show you how you might do more. Often the most difficult task is simply taking the first step. Perhaps you could talk with your pastor or another trusted friend about the opportunities that are open to you. You'll be surprised at the welcoming response you'll receive if you just ask, "Is there anything I can do to help?" Be confident that you are needed in the body of Christ, and take the risk of working with others to spread the kingdom of God. It's worth it!

"Father in heaven, thank you for the gifts and abilities that you have given me. Help me to join more closely with others in the work of Christian ministry."

So Much More Than a Personal Note

The Letter to Philemon

SO MUCH MORE THAN A PERSONAL NOTE

So Much More Than a Personal Note
An Introduction to the Letter to Philemon

by Leo Zanchettin

At first glance, we might wonder why such a short and seemingly private letter from St. Paul was included in the Bible. After all, Paul must have written many, many personal letters—both to close friends and to co-workers in other churches—during his nearly thirty-year career as an apostle. Yet none of those letters has been preserved. Surely this is not the only one of its kind that the early church had access to?

Of course, we do have letters Paul is said to have written to Timothy and Titus—again, personal letters to individual believers. But at least those letters touch on doctrinal issues and questions of church discipline. By contrast, the Letter to Philemon has nothing that sounds like teaching or advice on how to run a church. If anything, it gives us a glimpse into how Paul may have dealt with internal family issues. But even so, the question of how to treat a runaway slave would seem to have very little bearing on our everyday lives.

The oddity of this letter's presence in the New Testament canon has led some scholars to suggest that the slave mentioned in this letter, Onesimus, was freed by his master, Philemon, and went on to become a trusted coworker of Paul's and ultimately a bishop. According to this theory, because of his close relationship with Paul, Onesimus had a major hand in compiling the letters written by the apostle that would make their way into the developing New

Testament. Onesimus so treasured his freedom—and Paul's hand in it—that he might have included this letter as a tribute to the apostle.

This theory, while intriguing and even plausible, is ultimately unverifiable. It is also unnecessary as a justification for including the Letter to Philemon in the Bible. Many other people benefited from Paul's intervention, yet no written accounts of his goodness to them have been preserved. Rather than looking to personal influence or grateful remembrances, we would do better to look at the letter itself to discover its value and importance. If all Scripture is truly inspired by God and "useful for teaching, for reproof, for correction, and for training in righteousness" (2 Timothy 3:16), then we must look to this letter to discover how the Holy Spirit wants to speak to us.

Putting the Letter into Context. The first thing that a close reading of the Letter to Philemon reveals is that while the bulk of the letter is addressed to Philemon, the opening greeting envisions a much broader network of relationships. The letter is written by both Paul and Timothy (Philemon 1), and it is addressed not only to Philemon but to Apphia (probably Philemon's wife), to Archippus (a close friend?), and to the whole church that meets in Philemon's home (2). Philemon, it appears, is the leader of a small church community—at least a community small enough to conduct its liturgical gatherings in Philemon's home. While Paul's request to treat the wayward Onesimus with mercy and generosity is a personal one, he places his appeal in a much larger context. For Paul, Onesimus' situation is not simply a private, domestic issue but an issue of justice and mercy that touches the whole community of believers.

Since eight of the ten people named in this letter are also named in Paul's Letter to the Colossians, most scholars assume that Philemon lived in Colossae. Paul tells Philemon that he is writing from prison (Philemon 9), and this helps us locate Paul at the time of this letter as well. If Onesimus belongs to a household in Colossae, it is likely that he would not have traveled as far as Rome or Caesarea—two cities where Paul spent time in chains. The only other place in which we know Paul was imprisoned is Ephesus, which is about 120 miles away.

Paul and Onesimus. Paul wrote this letter because Onesimus, a slave owned by Philemon, had sought refuge or help from Paul, and Paul wanted to set the matter straight with Philemon. Whether Onesimus had run away in search of his freedom is not exactly clear from the letter, but it is unlikely. If he were an escapee, he would likely have been captured and forcibly returned to his master before reaching Ephesus. Another possibility is that Onesimus was a trusted member of Philemon's household and that on a journey (possibly to Ephesus) on behalf of his master, he lost some money or some other valuable item entrusted to him. Fearing Philemon's reaction, Onesimus sought out Paul for help.

Never one to waste an opportunity, Paul evangelized Onesimus and saw to it that he was baptized. This man who was once a stranger to Paul became his spiritual son (Philemon 10), and Paul grew to love him as a close brother in the Lord (12). Paul knew that it was illegal to hold another person's slave, and he also wanted to see the breach between Philemon and Onesimus remedied. So he sent Onesimus back home along with a letter asking Philemon to accept him again—only this time as a brother in Christ and not just as a slave (16). Where once Onesimus had been "useless" to Philemon—presumably because of his absence from his duties and perhaps due to whatever mistakes he had made—now he would prove himself more than useful (11).

The Question of Slavery. It is important to note that Paul is not necessarily asking Philemon to free Onesimus, even if the request may lie under the surface of the letter (Philemon 21). Some have read this letter, along with other Pauline passages such as Colossians 3:22-25 and 1 Corinthians 7:21-24 and faulted Paul for seeming to uphold the status quo and possibly even supporting the institution of slavery. But such an interpretation risks missing out on a broader dimension of Paul's approach to the gospel.

It is likely that Paul appreciated the injustice inherent in slavery but that he didn't advocate ending it because of the amount of time and energy such a project would entail. It has been suggested that as many as 30 percent of the empire's population was enslaved. It is also clear that slavery was an integral part of the economical and social structures of the Roman Empire. Consequently, its dismantling was unlikely at best—especially if it was called for by a small group that didn't even uphold the religion of the empire. Paul was never one to hesitate to confront injustices, but in the end he must have realized that it was simply inconceivable to take on the whole empire on this matter.

Given the situation, Paul must have concluded that it would be better to encourage slaves who have become Christians to take as "Christian" an approach to their situation as possible. For instance, in his Letter to the Colossians, he told slaves to work all the harder for their human masters, "as done for the Lord," knowing that the Lord would repay them by making them his heirs (Colossians 3:23-24). Taking such an approach had another benefit for slaves: their witness might help convert their masters—which might result in kinder treatment or even in their liberation. As for masters, Paul urged them to deal with their slaves with respect and kindness, since there was no partiality with God (Ephesians 6:9). So even if the entire institution of slavery could not be overturned immediately, at least a new dynamic could be introduced to it.

We see such an approach in this short letter of Paul's. Simply by casting Onesimus in the role of a brother and urging Philemon to accept this new relationship was revolutionary in itself (Philemon 15-16). To consider a slave a brother was unthinkable. Of course, some masters treated their slaves better than others, but there was never any question about slaves' status as pieces of commodity in a person's household. By contrast, the approach that Paul was urging on Philemon would upend such a view. Indeed, it could even produce an environment in which the concept of master and slave would gradually wither away.

A Letter about Brotherhood. This broader look at Paul's approach to Philemon gives us a better appreciation of the value that this short letter has for all ages and situations. In the end, the Letter to Philemon is not simply a note from one early Christian to another. Nor is it just a letter that touches on the issue of slavery. Ultimately, this letter is one of the New Testament's strongest witnesses to the transforming power of Christ and the radical nature of Christian brotherhood. For Philemon to accept Onesimus as a brother required nothing short of an inside-out renewal of his mind and heart. And for Paul to make his appeal solely on the basis of his brotherly relationship with Philemon rather than on the basis of his authority as an apostle shows how confident he was that this renewal would occur (Philemon 8-9).

Ultimately, this letter is all about God renewing the world through changed hearts. Even the most deeply rooted "truths" and traditions in us that stand in opposition to the gospel can be overturned. The promise of a new creation is not just theoretical. It is very real—and so very much filled with hope!

SO MUCH MORE THAN A PERSONAL NOTE

Philemon 1-7

¹ Paul, a prisoner of Christ Jesus, and Timothy our brother,

To Philemon our dear friend and co-worker, ²to Apphia our sister, to Archippus our fellow soldier, and to the church in your house:

³ Grace to you and peace from God our Father and the Lord Jesus Christ.

⁴ When I remember you in my prayers, I always thank my God ⁵because I hear of your love for all the saints and your faith toward the Lord Jesus. ⁶I pray that the sharing of your faith may become effective when you perceive all the good that we may do for Christ. ⁷I have indeed received much joy and encouragement from your love, because the hearts of the saints have been refreshed through you, my brother.

If you've ever been applauded for an effort you put your "heart and soul" into, then you can understand the power of praise. The admiration and appreciation of people who are important to us boosts our self-esteem and motivates us to continue doing our best. And even when there is room for improvement, being told that we really are championship material inspires us to become what others think we are capable of. So it is no wonder that Paul, who wanted to inspire Philemon to treat his slave Onesimus as a brother in Christ, began his letter with words of praise.

Paul shows his affection for Philemon when he tells Philemon that he remembers him in his prayers (Philemon 4). He praises Philemon for his love for the saints and his faith in Jesus. Paul shows that Philemon's spirituality is important when he says that he heard about it in prison and that he thanks God for it: "I always thank my God because I hear of your love for all the saints and your faith toward the Lord Jesus" (5).

Next Paul begins to inspire Philemon to do even more for Jesus, while at the same time he connects Philemon's efforts with his own. Paul's hope for Philemon is sacred and solemn because it is expressed as a prayer: "I pray that the sharing of your faith may become effective when you perceive all the good that *we* may do for Christ" (Philemon 6). Paul will go on to show Philemon a particular good that he wants him to perceive—namely that he should change his treatment of Onesimus. But first he closes this paragraph with more praise for Philemon, whom he affectionately refers to as his "brother"— this time by telling Philemon how good his love has made him feel and how much it has done for the people of God: "I have indeed received much joy and encouragement from your love, because the hearts of the saints have been refreshed through you, my brother" (7).

It is not surprising that Paul's words in this brief introduction would have disposed Philemon to favorably receive Paul's upcoming request, about which Paul says, "[T]hough I am bold enough in Christ to command you to do your duty, yet I would rather appeal to you on the basis of love" (Philemon 8-9). The love that Paul declared for Philemon would likely have made him want to continue to please Paul. At the end of the letter, Paul inspires Philemon to even go beyond his request, when he expresses his assurance of what Philemon is capable of doing: "Confident of your obedience, I am writing to you, knowing that you will do even more than I say" (21).

Paul's praise inspired Philemon to do good work for Christ. And we all know how praise can motivate us. Let's not miss opportunities to encourage those around us by praising them for the good they do. By recognizing the efforts of our family members, our co-workers, and our friends, as well as by showing confidence in what we believe they are capable of, we can help them to reach the full potential of what God calls them to be.

"Thank you, Lord, for the love and confidence you have shown in me. Help me to inspire others and give them confidence through my words of praise and encouragement."

Philemon 7-21

[7] I have indeed received much joy and encouragement from your love, because the hearts of the saints have been refreshed through you, my brother. [8] For this reason, though I am bold enough in Christ to command you to do your duty, [9]yet I would rather appeal to you on the basis of love—and I, Paul, do this as an old man, and now also as a prisoner of Christ Jesus. [10]I am appealing to you for my child, Onesimus, whose father I have become during my imprisonment. [11]Formerly he was useless to you, but now he is indeed useful both to you and to me. [12]I am sending him, that is, my own heart, back to you. [13]I wanted to keep him with me, so that he might be of service to me in your place during my imprisonment for the gospel; [14]but I preferred to do nothing without your consent, in order that your good deed might be voluntary and not something forced. [15]Perhaps this is the reason he was separated from you for a while, so that you might have him back forever, [16]no longer as a slave but more than a slave, a beloved brother—especially to me but how much more to you, both in the flesh and in the Lord. [17] So if you consider me your partner, welcome him as you would welcome me. [18]If he has wronged you in any way, or owes you any-

thing, charge that to my account. [19]I, Paul, am writing this with my own hand: I will repay it. I say nothing about your owing me even your own self. [20]Yes, brother, let me have this benefit from you in the Lord! Refresh my heart in Christ. [21]Confident of your obedience, I am writing to you, knowing that you will do even more than I say.

While a prisoner in Rome, Paul wrote this warm personal letter to Philemon, a fellow Christian and owner of the slave Onesimus. Onesimus had fled from his master earlier and gone to Rome, where he was converted through Paul's ministry. Paul wanted the slave to return to Philemon and sent this letter along, perhaps via Tychicus, who was to accompany Onesimus (Colossians 4:7-9).

Slavery was an acceptable part of the culture of the time, and Paul did not attack it as an institution, as we might expect from our modern-day perspective. Small Christian communities scattered throughout the Roman Empire were in no position to do so. Instead, Paul took a position that was quite revolutionary for those times. He asked his friend to receive Onesimus back, not as a slave but as a beloved brother in Christ (Philemon 16). Paul saw how unity in the body of Christ cut across worldly position, occupation, socioeconomic status, race, and nationality. "There is no longer Jew or Greek, there is no longer slave or free, there is no longer male and female; for all of you are one in Christ Jesus" (Galatians 3:28).

Today, we have been called to this same unity in the body of Christ. Though slavery is not part of our cultural pattern, division and prejudice can dominate relationships in our schools, our parishes, our jobs, and even our families. In many ways, deeply held prejudices may be subtle. If we ask the Spirit to probe us, however, we may come to see how we separate ourselves from others simply because of their race, nationality, occupation, educational background, or economic status.

Paul encouraged Philemon to see Onesimus as his brother in Christ. We too must see each other in the same way—as brothers and sisters in Christ. Jesus' death on the cross has reconciled us to the Father and enables us to be united in him (Ephesians 2:16). The Holy Spirit can make this truth real, giving us the ability to see one another in terms of heavenly unity rather than by worldly standards.

"Lord Jesus, through your cross you showed us the extent of your desire for us to be one in your body. Through your Spirit, teach us how we can care for one another with this same love so that the unity of your body will be evident to all."

Philemon 22-25

22 One thing more—prepare a guest room for me, for I am hoping through your prayers to be restored to you.
23 Epaphras, my fellow prisoner in Christ Jesus, sends greetings to you, 24and so do Mark, Aristarchus, Demas, and Luke, my fellow workers.
25 The grace of the Lord Jesus Christ be with your spirit.

S t. Paul closes this letter to his dear friend Philemon by praying, "The grace of the Lord Jesus Christ be with your spirit." It sounds so formulaic, but if we consider the context of this verse, we can see that Paul had more in mind than a simple farewell.

Paul knew that it would be by the grace of God that Philemon would be able to overcome whatever doubts he had about his former slave Onesimus and receive him back as a brother in Christ. Paul also knew that without the comfort and assurance that come from God, Philemon would find it a lot more difficult to adapt to a new way of relating to Onesimus.

Grace works like that in us, too. It helps us do things, think things, and believe things that we could not otherwise do on our own. The *Catechism of the Catholic Church* defines grace this way: "Grace is *favor*, the *free and undeserved help* that God gives us to respond to his call to become children of God, adoptive sons, partakers of the divine nature and of eternal life" (1996). In other words, when the grace of Jesus Christ is at work in our spirits, we can live beyond our normal human capacities.

As in the case of Philemon, grace is especially important in the work of healing and forgiveness. It is not easy to forgive those who have hurt us, especially those who have deeply wronged us. Yet Jesus does call us to forgive, and he would never call us to something that he was not prepared to empower us to do. It may not be easy, but it is possible as we look to the Spirit for the power to do what seems impossible. Likewise, it is not easy to love everyone, especially our enemies. Yet once again, Jesus calls us to love without condition or prejudice (Matthew 5:44). Impossible? Not with the grace of God!

Today may be a good day to examine whether you are carrying around a burden of unforgiveness, or to identify people that you find so hard to love. Today just may be the day when you receive a special infilling from the Spirit that lifts you up and softens your heart.

Whether or not you "feel" anything, you can be absolutely sure that your prayer has been heard and that God has acted! Jesus will never call you to do something that you cannot do. Trust Jesus, and he will act.

"Lord Jesus, fill me with your grace so that I can be more like you: a friend of sinners, a forgiver of wrongdoers, and a lover of enemies."

Meeting the Challenge of Change

The Letter to the Hebrews

Meeting the Challenge of Change

Meeting the Challenge of Change
An Introduction to the Letter to the Hebrews

by Fr. Joseph A. Mindling, OFM Cap

T he Letter to the Hebrews offers readers in the first half of the twenty-first century a fascinating window into the spiritual life of the church in the second half of the first century. In this letter, we capture a sense of how first- and second-generation believers in Christ received crucial new insights as they reflected on the meaning and implications of Jesus' ongoing role in their lives. But this text offers us more than an engaging history lesson. Reading it ourselves, we too can be enlightened and encouraged by the same words that helped the early church negotiate the transition from a rich religious past into an even more noble future.

An Ancient but Elusive Masterpiece. From the beginning of Christian history, this text has been recognized and esteemed in a special way. Quotations borrowed from it already appear in writings as early as the letters of Pope St. Clement I, one of Peter's earliest successors at the end of the first century. Very early on, passages from Hebrews also found their way into the church's liturgy—and have been there ever since. Still, despite this letter's popularity and influence, we know very little about when and where it was written and who wrote it.

Early collections of New Testament writings frequently positioned Hebrews right after the letters attributed to Paul, and this custom is still followed today. However, the ancient traditions in the East and West are far from unanimous about whether, or to what degree, St. Paul was the source of its ideas or its actual wording. Significant dissimilarities in style and content between Hebrews and the letters attributed to Paul have resulted in a rather solid consensus among Catholics and Protestants today that Paul did not write Hebrews.

Other candidates (Barnabas, Apollos, Aquila, and Priscilla, just to mention a few) have also been proposed, but without winning any serious or widespread support. Most modern scholars tend now to agree with Origen, the third-century biblical scholar who concluded that "only God knows" who his inspired human coauthor was.

Interpreting an Ancient Title. Among the first things about this writing that may catch our attention are the two particular terms in the title: "letter" and "Hebrews." The thirteen "letters" located right before this one in the New Testament all begin, as any ancient letter would, with the names both of the writer and of the intended recipients. So we may wonder why no such information is supplied at the beginning of this "letter." And then, how is it that a composition situated right in the middle of the most explicitly Christian part of the Bible looks as if it is directed primarily toward a Jewish readership?

What may have prompted ancient copyists to refer to this writing as a letter was probably the fact that its closing paragraphs do sound very much like the way people often concluded letters in the first century. And, in manuscript form, it could have easily been considered letter-size, since its length is somewhere between that of First and Second Corinthians. Nevertheless, the strongly rhetorical style of the opening verses, along with the tone and content of the text as a whole, indicate that it would be more accurate to describe Hebrews as a written homily designed to both instruct and exhort, or, as the New American Bible translates it, "a message of encouragement."

As far as the phrase "to the Hebrews" is concerned, we know that the headings used as titles in modern Bibles often date back to editorial captions provided by those who hand-copied Scriptures as they were first being preserved. Although these titles are not actually part of the inspired text, they do testify to revered traditions. In this case, the antiquity of its language calls for the term "Hebrews" to be taken not in the modern sense of "Jewish readers" but rather as the term was used in the early church—as a reference to believers who had been raised as Jews and who had then become converts to Christianity. The intended recipients, then, were Jewish Christians.

This means that a familiarity with the religious world of our Jewish-Christian ancestors is an important key to unlocking many of the ideas and images in Hebrews—especially its extensive "rabbinical" use of the Hebrew Scriptures. Beyond that, however, it is also important to remember that in the first decades after Jesus' ascension, embracing the gospel did not necessarily mean immediately relinquishing many expressions of Judaism. So as we read this letter, we need to reflect on the effects that this practice had in the period leading up to its composition.

Meeting the Challenge of Change. In the Acts of the Apostles, Luke shows how St. Peter, although already active as a Christian leader and missionary, could hardly bring himself to eat nonkosher foods, to enter the homes of prospective converts if they were pagans, or even to share a common table with baptized persons of gentile origin. Eventually he managed to change both his behavior and his thinking regarding all of these issues, but the fact that this "pillar of the church" needed to work through these stages of conversion highlights how big the challenge was.

Luke also reports that in the days after Pentecost, Peter and John continued to attend daily prayers in the Temple in Jerusalem. How could they do that, knowing that such activities were conducted under the authority of the same high priestly families who had successfully plotted Jesus' death? As late as the fifties Paul, too, let himself be persuaded to take part in a religious vow ceremony in the same temple. Could he have been indifferent to the fact that such activities involved collaborating with the Jewish priests who presided at them?

Paul's missionary accomplishments throughout the gentile world were sometimes seriously compromised by interlopers who tried to cajole gentile converts to adopt traditional Jewish practices—all of which Paul and other church leaders had declared unnecessary. Yet at the same time, Paul himself had insisted that his young co-worker Timothy, who came from a practicing Jewish family, be circumcised before he could join him in full-time evangelization.

All of these "New Testament snapshots" show that the early Christian community needed to rethink its own essential character and its relationship with those who also considered themselves "children of Abraham" but rejected Jesus as the Son of God. Emerging from this background, the Letter to the Hebrews is best understood as a record documenting a dramatic coming to consciousness. It contains the most explicit witness we have to the theological reasoning that prompted Jewish Christians to reexamine what it meant that Jesus is the priestly mediator of the new covenant.

Content and Thought Flow. The following summary of the principal teachings of Hebrews can help us identify the main points developed in its thirteen short but compact chapters. A more detailed account would need to devote much more attention than space permits here to the kaleidoscope of Old Testament passages that enrich every section. However, the best way to gain a personal appreciation of that dimension is through repeated attentive readings and dedicated, prayerful meditation. That, of course, is what we hope to accomplish in the meditations that follow this introduction.

An Icon Painted with Words. With majestic rhetoric, the opening paragraph greets the reader with a striking description of Christ enthroned triumphantly at the right hand of God. First, he is presented as the Father's perfect counterpart and only worthy heir. The universe was created through Christ and is also sustained in existence through him. Next, he is presented as the one who purifies us of sin and who constitutes the pinnacle of God's revelation of himself down through the ages. Finally, his divinely proclaimed sonship is shown to be eternal, and his unique status as "the firstborn brought into the world" makes him far superior even to the angels (Hebrews 1:1-14).

If God's former messages to us, delivered by heavenly messengers, made us aware of the impact of divine justice on the human stage, it is all the more important that we focus our attention on the promise of salvation he has announced in and through Christ (Hebrews 2:1-4). God's plan is to set humankind over all creation, and though this may seem a far-from-realized goal at present, Jesus has already led the way to this exaltation. By participating fully in our nature, even to the point of suffering and dying, he has been able to overcome the threat of death. By becoming totally "brother" to us, he has made himself the perfectly accessible priest, capable of understanding our side of the relationship with complete compassion and empathy (2:5-18).

An Image to Inspire Trust. Although Moses was a great broker between God and the people, Jesus is a far more capable and effective intercessor for us. Still, we must commit ourselves resolutely to accepting his invitation to holiness in order to share in his effectiveness. As an important reminder that we too can drift away or become complacent, the author recalls the unfaithfulness of many among the chosen people who fell away after the Exodus. But Jesus, the "Joshua of the New Covenant," will lead us into the rest that is the Promised Land if we remain confidently docile to the all-seeing, all-penetrating word of God (Hebrews 3:1–4:13).

The author then goes on to reflect on Jesus' role as our high priest as an important and effective way to reinvigorate our faith and to encourage us to take advantage of how approachable Jesus is. Of course, he remains the supreme mediator on high, but he is still always present and available to each one of us.

According to the "Order of Melchizedek." The author next demonstrates the excellence of Jesus' priesthood by comparing it to the priestly service that had come before it. The Aaronic-Levitical priesthood of Judaism enjoyed the endorsement of the covenant that was spelled out in the Pentateuch. But in practice, this priesthood was imperfect in several ways. Under the original law, priests were sinners who needed to offer sacrifices for themselves as well as for the offenses of the people. They also had to be continually replaced since, like every other mortal human being, they too died. Most important, their service was ultimately defective because it did not compensate for moral offenses and was not capable of eradicating the *power* of sin.

Under the new covenant, the appointment of a high priest still needed God's approval, and this was willingly granted even though Jesus did not seek this honor for himself. However, a dramatic shift is now introduced. Interestingly, it is at this point that the author expresses concern and uncertainty about whether some of his readers will be unable to accept or even understand what he is about to explain (Hebrews 6:1-12).

Unlike the model followed in the Old Testament, Jesus was not an automatic candidate for priestly office on the grounds that he was born into the tribe of Levi. Instead, as the anointed heir of the house of David, he is identified with the unnamed person addressed in Psalm 110:4: "The LORD has sworn and he will not reverse himself. You are a priest forever, according to the order of Melchizedek."

This mysterious figure called Melchizedek is depicted in Genesis 14:18-20 as superior to Abraham himself. We see this in the way Abraham showed deference to Melchizedek by taking advantage of his priestly service and by paying him tithes (Hebrews 6:13–7:19).

Two further hallmarks confirm that the priesthood of Christ is in a class by itself. First, the wording in the psalm speaks of an oath, a mode of divine appointment that no Old Testament priest ever received. Second, what Jesus offered through his death on the cross was the perfect sacrifice, and as such, it needed to be performed only once. The author also comments that it is only appropriate for Jesus to exercise a higher priesthood. The new covenant that he inaugurated is, after all, superior to the original covenant in which the Levitical priests functioned (Hebrews 7:20–8:12).

Beyond the Past into the New Order. By implication, then, the old covenant has not been rendered invalid, but rather, obsolete. Its sanctuary, priesthood, and system of sacrifices were effectively replaced when Jesus offered himself as the perfect victim for the forgiveness of sin. Only he was worthy of entering the real Holy of Holies in heaven. Believers who really understand what Jesus' priestly ministry involves must now see that participation in the old system is no longer a viable option for Christians (Hebrews 8:13–10:18).

The author then tells us how this understanding of the new covenant in Christ should move us to approach Jesus with eager confidence, knowing that his blood can cleanse us of all sin. It should also draw us to join together with our fellow believers on a regular basis to give and receive encouragement so that we can all persevere in faith, hope, and love. By contrast, to see the truth of the new covenant and then to spurn it brings about a divine retribution even more severe than the consequences visited upon those who violated the original covenant. Hence the author invites his readers to recall the sufferings that they had already endured and to persevere to the end, so that they will not lose out on its promised rewards (Hebrews 10:19-39).

This monumental transition in salvation history that Jesus brought about requires some painful letting go of old ways of thinking and acting. But at the same time, the author recognizes an important continuity with the Hebrew Scriptures: He urges us to continue in the faith that the heroes and heroines had "in things unseen," a faith that pleased God and won his approval in their lives. The impressive list presented in Chapter 11 of models of confident reliance on God's word includes many well-known names, but it also refers to many more anonymous figures—a great cloud of witnesses that climaxes with Jesus himself, the "pioneer and perfecter of our faith" (Hebrews 11:1–12:3).

A Final Look. The greetings and blessing that conclude the Letter to the Hebrews come just after a potpourri of moral concerns that touch briefly on a wide variety of subjects. One can easily imagine that if the cautions and exhortations included here were presented in a modern pastoral letter, they could well be cast into a long list of "discussion questions."

Still drawing on many examples from Scripture, the author raises many thought-provoking topics that can be understood as practical applications of the rich theological teachings laid out in the earlier chapters (Hebrews 12:4–13:23). So whether he is urging us to "let mutual love continue," to be careful not to be carried away by "all kinds of strange teachings," or to "do good and share what [we] have," the call is always to live in the freedom and the hope of the new covenant that Jesus has inaugurated for us. By his blood we are set free from sin and invited to enter the heavenly sanctuary every day "with a true heart in full assurance of faith" (10:22).

MEETING THE CHALLENGE OF CHANGE

Hebrews 1:1-6

1 Long ago God spoke to our ancestors in many and various ways by the prophets, 2but in these last days he has spoken to us by a Son, whom he appointed heir of all things, through whom he also created the worlds. 3He is the reflection of God's glory and the exact imprint of God's very being, and he sustains all things by his powerful word. When he had made purification for sins, he sat down at the right hand of the Majesty on high, 4having become as much superior to angels as the name he has inherited is more excellent than theirs.

5 For to which of the angels did God ever say,
> "You are my Son;
>> today I have begotten you"?

Or again,
> "I will be his Father,
>> and he will be my Son"?

6And again, when he brings the firstborn into the world, he says,
> "Let all God's angels worship him."

The Letter to the Hebrews begins with this marvelous statement: "Long ago God spoke to our ancestors in many and various ways by the prophets, but in these last days he has spoken to us by a Son, whom he appointed heir of all things, through whom he also created the worlds" (Hebrews 1:1-2). What a wonderfully compact statement of the gospel message! Too bad we don't know who wrote it!

Hebrews has always been a bit of a mystery to commentators. Many early church writers saw in it the influence of a Pharisee like Paul because the letter depends so heavily on quotes from the Old Testament. But its style is totally different from Paul's other works. Other scholars claimed that the writer was Paul's coevangelist, Barnabas, "the son of encouragement" (Acts 4:36). Indeed, Hebrews is unsurpassed in its exhortation to faith. And even though debate continues—others have proposed Luke, Apollos, and even the deaconess Priscilla—the letter has always been accepted as authentically inspired by the Holy Spirit. An early pope, Clement of Rome, even quoted Hebrews around the year 96 A.D.

Modern scholarship reveals a well-composed epistle, dating most likely from before 67 A.D. Although the intended audience is never identified, no doubt tradition is correct in pointing to a community made up chiefly of Jewish Christians rooted in the Hebrew religious culture and language. Beyond that, we know it is an exciting letter with a powerful, timeless message: Fix your eyes on Jesus, the Son of God and the fulfillment of Yahweh's age-old promise to his people.

Hebrews is infused with an experiential knowledge of Jesus' identity and his great power to deliver us from all bondage. He is our "great high priest" (Hebrews 4:14) who constantly intercedes for us (7:25), and whose blood was shed to cleanse our consciences (9:14). He is the author and perfecter of our faith (12:2) who continually sustains not only our lives, but the entire universe as well (1:3). Jesus can deal with every fear, every sin, every obstacle in our life of faith. He can give us every reason to "hold fast to the confession of our hope without wavering, for he who has promised is faithful" (10:23).

"Son of God, you faced death for our sake so that we could be reunited into the family of God. May my life glorify you today."

Hebrews 1:7-14

[7]Of the angels he says,
> "He makes his angels winds,
>> and his servants flames of fire."

[8]But of the Son he says,
> "Your throne, O God, is forever and ever,
>> and the righteous scepter is the scepter of your kingdom.

[9] You have loved righteousness and hated wickedness;
> therefore God, your God, has anointed you
>> with the oil of gladness beyond your companions."

[10]And,
> "In the beginning, Lord, you founded the earth,
>> and the heavens are the work of your hands;

[11] they will perish, but you remain;
>> they will all wear out like clothing;

[12] like a cloak you will roll them up,
>> and like clothing they will be changed.
> But you are the same,
>> and your years will never end."

[13]But to which of the angels has he ever said,
> "Sit at my right hand
>> until I make your enemies a footstool for your feet"?

[14]Are not all angels spirits in the divine service, sent to serve for the sake of those who are to inherit salvation?

J ust as the author of the Letter to the Hebrews is unknown, the people who first received the letter are something of a mystery, too: They aren't even formally addressed as a church! And unlike the Romans or Corinthians, we do not know much about the life situation of these anonymous "Hebrews."

That they were Jewish Christians seems obvious, of course, partly because the letter relies so heavily on Old Testament references. Take this passage, for example. In the short space of a few lines, the writer pieced together quotations from several different psalms to emphasize the supremacy of Christ. Jesus is "anointed with the oil of gladness" (Hebrews 1:9) and sits on the throne of God (1:8). Clearly the writer relied on his audience's mutual knowledge and reverence for Scripture to reaffirm the community's faith that Jesus was the Messiah who fulfilled the law and the prophets.

Another characteristic that emerges from the text was that the Hebrews were in a serious struggle. The specific circumstances are not clear, but the author is compelled again and again to challenge their lack of faith. They "have become dull in understanding" (Hebrews 5:11) the gospel. They showed a tendency to "neglect" the great salvation of Christ (2:3). To persevere, they needed encouragement— and that is the watchword of this letter.

Consequently, the author, acting as a true pastor of souls, filled the letter with exhortations. He reminds the Hebrews that God is always faithful to his promises. Humans may waver and change their minds— some may even fall away—but God's love remains the same. The imagery taken from Psalm 102 was meant to remind them—and us today as well—that even though heaven and earth will "wear out like a garment," God remains "the same" (Hebrews 1:11-12, Psalm 102:26).

The universal message for us from this letter is that we can be steadfast in a God who never changes in his love for us. In spite of our inconstant faith and our sinfulness, God remains committed to caring for us and to bringing us to salvation. The author summed it up later in the letter: "Jesus Christ is the same yesterday and today and forever" (Hebrews 13:8). In every age, we can depend on this truth, no matter what the circumstances of our lives.

"Father, today I surrender my life to you. I marvel that you have called me to yourself in Christ. I am amazed that you have anointed me with 'the oil of gladness'!"

Hebrews 2:1-4

[1] Therefore we must pay greater attention to what we have heard, so that we do not drift away from it. [2]For if the message declared through angels was valid, and every transgression or disobedience received a just penalty, [3]how can we escape if we neglect so great a salvation? It was declared at first through the Lord, and it was attested to us by those who heard him, [4]while God added his testimony by signs and wonders and various miracles, and by gifts of the Holy Spirit, distributed according to his will.

Three small words from this passage demonstrate that a skilled and loving pastor was behind the Letter to the Hebrews: "drift," "neglect," and "we."

The first word that catches our attention is "drift": "We must pay greater attention to what we have heard, so that we do not *drift* away from it" (Hebrews 2:1). By using a nautical term, the author metaphorically compares the people to a boat that has slipped from its mooring and begins to drift away with the tide. A better knot or a more secure line could have prevented the boat from drifting. To allow such a thing to happen is almost worse than if someone had stolen the boat.

Next, this sense of wastefulness and loss is reinforced by the word "neglect": "How can we escape if we *neglect* so great a salvation?" (Hebrews 2:3). Again, carelessness comes to mind. People who neglect their salvation are not deliberately setting their minds to turn away from God. They are simply allowing themselves to drift away like the lost boat. They do not plan to sin, but they allow distractions—hobbies, work, the television, and a great many other things—to get in the way.

Of course, you cannot neglect something unless you first have it! The author reminds the Hebrews: You have tasted the salvation of Christ! This is a marvelous truth, but at the same time what a great tragedy if this life with God is snuffed out through negligence.

Hebrews tells us that action and focus are the remedy for such neglect. Throughout the letter, the writer calls his flock to "pay greater attention" (Hebrews 2:1) to God's word, and to "consider" Jesus (3:1;12:3). The Hebrews—and we ourselves—are called to "fix our thoughts" on what we have already heard and experienced: that God loves us and that Christ has saved us.

Finally, the author declares "we" are in this together: "Therefore *we* must pay greater attention to what *we* have heard, so that *we* do not drift away from it" (Hebrews 2:1). With this simple pronoun, the author throws his lot in with the readers. It signals their solidarity as brothers and sisters in Christ, a fellowship in following the Lord.

Today, let us safeguard our minds against temptation. Let us cherish the time we spend with the Lord in personal prayer, at Mass, and in pondering his word. Let us be grateful for the "signs and wonders" (Hebrews 2:4) that God has performed in our lives.

"Lord, you have been so good to me! You have rescued me from sin, and every day you continue to minister to me. By your Spirit, help me to stand firm against temptation. Jesus, I don't want to slip away from you!"

Hebrews 2:5-13

5 Now God did not subject the coming world, about which we are speaking, to angels. 6But someone has testified somewhere,

> "What are human beings that you are mindful of them,
>> or mortals, that you care for them?

7 You have made them for a little while lower than the angels;
> you have crowned them with glory and honor,

8 subjecting all things under their feet."

Now in subjecting all things to them, God left nothing outside their control. As it is, we do not yet see everything in subjection to them, 9but we do see Jesus, who for a little while was made lower than the angels, now crowned with glory and honor because of the suffering of death, so that by the grace of God he might taste death for everyone.
10 It was fitting that God, for whom and through whom all things exist, in bringing many children to glory, should make the pioneer of their salvation perfect through sufferings. 11For the one who sanctifies and those who are sanctified all have one Father. For this reason Jesus is not ashamed to call them brothers and sisters, 12saying,

> "I will proclaim your name to my brothers and sisters,
>> in the midst of the congregation I will praise you."

13And again,

> "I will put my trust in him."

And again,

"Here am I and the children
whom God has given me."

As it is, we do not yet see everything in subjection to them,
but we do see Jesus. —Hebrews 2:8-9

Psalm 8, which the author of Hebrews refers to in this passage, depicts humanity as being chosen by God to have dominion over all creation. The author observes that as of yet, this hasn't happened—*but* that we do see Jesus—the head of all humanity—crowned in glory and honor. In other words, while we are still subject to sickness, suffering, and death, Jesus has triumphed. And, in him, we can all see our destiny fulfilled.

"We see Jesus" (Hebrews 2:9). You can almost hear the writer of Hebrews crying out, "Fix your eyes on Jesus! See him crowned as head of humanity! Since you share the same Father in heaven, you are part of his family. Jesus' conquest over death is applicable to you as well. As head of our race, he leads the way and promises us that we will share in his victory!"

Something life giving happens when we fix our eyes on Jesus. Picturing him in all his glory and honor can move us to praise and thank him for giving us a share in his victory. As we gaze upon the risen Christ in prayer and at Mass, our problems, infirmities, and even our struggles with sin become less prominent in our minds. The Holy Spirit broadens our perspective, and impenetrable mountains of difficulties become manageable molehills. Sometimes we even see a divine wisdom that we would not have seen otherwise.

In prayer today, take time to free your mind from the details of every-day life. Turn your mind to Jesus instead. See him crowned in glory and honor because he tasted death for you and everyone else. Your problems may not go away, but through time in prayer you can receive revelation from God that strengthens and encourages you. More than just warming our hearts, revelation can heal our minds and free us from the fears and the mind-sets that are part of life in this world.

"Lord Jesus, open my eyes to see you in all your splendor. You are the head of humanity, and yet you call me to participate in your glory. Help me always to look to you and to set my mind on the victory you have won for me."

Hebrews 2:14-18

[14] Since, therefore, the children share flesh and blood, he himself likewise shared the same things, so that through death he might destroy the one who has the power of death, that is, the devil, [15]and free those who all their lives were held in slavery by the fear of death. [16]For it is clear that he did not come to help angels, but the descendants of Abraham. [17]Therefore he had to become like his brothers and sisters in every respect, so that he might be a merciful and faithful high priest in the service of God, to make a sacrifice of atonement for the sins of the people. [18]Because he himself was tested by what he suffered, he is able to help those who are being tested.

W hen the author of Hebrews wrote that "he did not come to help angels, but the descendants of Abraham" (Hebrews 2:16), he chose a verb (*epitambano* in Greek) that literally means "to take hold of." In other words, by becoming one like us, Jesus has "taken hold of" the human race, embracing the fullness of our human condition and raising us up to be united with him in heaven.

Jesus' life, as fully God and fully man, reveals the gentle way that he wants to take hold of us. He came into this world not as a glorious king or mighty warrior, but as a humble baby born into a poor family. Rather than grasping us by violent force or overwhelming us with a magnificent display of power, he humbled himself; he shared in our nature, inviting us to follow him (Hebrews 2:14).

Jesus did not take hold of us in order to condemn us or chastise us. He came to free us from sin, to give us his life, to make us his brothers and sisters. Recall how he grasped Peter who was sinking in the water (Matthew 14:30-31) and the way he took hold of a man's shriveled hand to heal it (Matthew 12:10-13). Jesus constantly sought to take hold of people and lead them to the Father's love and compassion.

When Jesus died on the cross, he held on to each of us, taking us with him through death into resurrection. At his ascension, he still held on to us, desiring with all his heart that we would join him. From his heavenly throne, he sent the Holy Spirit so that we could daily experience his hand upon us. Jesus has a perfect plan for our lives, and he never has—and never will—let us go.

We can trust that Jesus' hand is still upon us today. When we read Scripture, worship him at Mass, care for our children—even when we sleep—we can count on the fact that Jesus is with us, waiting for us to turn to him.

"Lord Jesus, help us understand more deeply that you have held us in your heart since before time began. As we live each day, help us to be more aware of your presence and more confident that we can share in your eternal life."

Hebrews 3:1-6

[1] Therefore, brothers and sisters, holy partners in a heavenly calling, consider that Jesus, the apostle and high priest of our confession, [2]was faithful to the one who appointed him, just as Moses also "was faithful in all God's house." [3]Yet Jesus is worthy of more glory than Moses, just as the builder of a house has more honor than the house itself. [4](For every house is built by someone, but the builder of all things is God.) [5]Now Moses was faithful in all God's house as a servant, to testify to the things that would be spoken later. [6]Christ, however, was faithful over God's house as a son, and we are his house if we hold firm the confidence and the pride that belong to hope.

In this passage, the author calls Jesus the "high priest of our confession" (3:1). This term—*archierus* in the original Greek—is the title most often given to Jesus throughout the Letter to the Hebrews (Hebrews 2:17; 3:1; 4:14, 15; 5:5, 10; 6:20; 7:26; 8:1; 9:11). Not only does the author use this title for Jesus more than any other, but he is also the *only* New Testament author who calls Jesus our high priest.

The author understood that under the Law of Moses, the high priest was an intermediary selected from among ordinary human beings "to offer gifts and sacrifices for sins" (Hebrews 5:1). In Judaism, as in many other religions, the function of the priesthood is to form a link between humanity and God. And in Jesus, this link is stronger and more intimate than anyone could have possibly imagined: Jesus' ministry as *our* high priest is tied directly with the reality that he is both Son of God and a human just like us.

Because Jesus is at the same time both man and God, he is the perfect priest. He represents God to humanity, and humanity to God. When the Father looks at us, he sees Jesus and the perfect sacrifice that purifies all of us and gives us access to the throne of God. And when the Father looks at Jesus, he sees reflected in his Son all the sons and daughters he has made in his image and likeness.

The author associates Jesus' priesthood with the notion that his ministry has surpassed everything in the old covenant. Comparing Jesus to Moses, who established the Law of Israel, the author states that Jesus is worthy of "more glory than Moses, just as the builder of a house has more honor than the house itself" (Hebrews 3:2-3). Even as he points his readers to Jesus' true nature as eternal priest, the author calls to mind *our* true nature as "holy partners in a heavenly calling" (3:1). He goes even further, calling us the house of Christ: "We are his house if we hold firm the confidence and the pride that belong to hope" (3:6).

How do we "hold firm"? The clue is in the first sentence of this passage: We must "consider" our high priest, Jesus. This term, *consider*, can be translated "to fix our thoughts" on Jesus. If we treasure Jesus in our hearts just as Mary and all the saints did, we will be moved to hold firm to our high status as Jesus' very partners on earth. So today, turn to Jesus, who bridges heaven and earth.

"Lord, you made it possible for me to answer a heavenly calling that is impossible to embrace on my own. Through your Holy Spirit, give me the strength today to follow you to the Father's heart."

Hebrews 3:7-14

7 Therefore, as the Holy Spirit says,
"Today, if you hear his voice,
8 do not harden your hearts as in the rebellion,
as on the day of testing in the wilderness,
9 where your ancestors put me to the test,
though they had seen my works [10]for forty years.
Therefore I was angry with that generation,
and I said, 'They always go astray in their hearts,
and they have not known my ways.'
11 As in my anger I swore,
'They will not enter my rest.'"

[12]Take care, brothers and sisters, that none of you may have an evil, unbelieving heart that turns away from the living God. [13]But exhort one another every day, as long as it is called "today," so that none of you may be hardened by the deceitfulness of sin. [14]For we have become partners of Christ, if only we hold our first confidence firm to the end.

The "rest" of God (Hebrews 3:11). It sounds so appealing—no worries or cares, no pain or suffering. Yet, is this a true representation? In the Old Testament, God's "rest" spoke of the promise God made to the Israelites who followed him as he commanded them; they would be free from wars, battles, and famine. This rest was a symbol of liberation, where they could be free to set their hearts on Yahweh and to be joined to him as his beloved people. For the writer of Hebrews, God's rest implies even more. It is the ultimate destiny of every Christian in heaven—a reward we share in Christ "if only we hold our first confidence firm to the end"(3:14).

What is our way into this rest? Over and over again, Scripture presents us with the perfect example of Jesus, whose humility and faithfulness to the Father brought him peace. Does this mean we must achieve Christ-like perfection if we want to enter into God's rest? If so, we would have no hope. The struggles to obey our own standards of righteousness—let alone God's law—are enough to overwhelm us! We all have been in numerous situations in which we felt stretched beyond our limits and far from the peace of God's rest.

God's call is challenging; there is no doubt about that. At the same time, however, he calls us to rely on Jesus' perfect work of ushering us into God's presence through the shedding of his blood. We are not capable of attaining his rest through rules of life or a formula. But we can attain his rest through belief in Christ as our atonement for sin and through the power of the indwelling Spirit. Thanks be to God!

While this rest is our future destiny as Christians, it is also a present reality every day as we commit ourselves to the Lord. Every day, Jesus invites us, "Come to me, all you that are weary and are carrying heavy burdens, and I will give you rest" (Matthew 11:28). His peace is a gift to us! Jesus gave his life that we would become children of God, a people after his own heart—embraced by him, filled with his love, empowered by his Spirit. Let us respond to his gracious invitation and in faith enter into his rest both now and more completely when we meet him face-to-face.

"Jesus, help me to commit my life to you. Let me rely on you as the key to my salvation. Send me the gift of your Spirit so that I may fully respond to your invitation to enter your rest."

Hebrews 3:15-19

¹⁵As it is said,

"Today if you hear his voice,

do not harden your hearts as in the rebellion."

¹⁶ Now who were they who heard and yet were rebellious? Was it not all those who left Egypt under the leadership of Moses? ¹⁷But with whom was he angry forty years? Was it not those who sinned, whose bodies fell in the wilderness? ¹⁸And to whom did he swear that they would not enter his rest, if not to those who were disobedient? ¹⁹So we see that they were unable to enter because of unbelief.

Hebrews has been called a letter of encouragement, but what does the word "encouragement" really mean? Encouragement does not mean just making someone feel good. Instead, it challenges us to grow and persevere even against difficult obstacles. In the process, the letter necessarily deals with some harsh realities. But it shows the early Christians—and us today—the way to deal with those realities in order to attain salvation.

For example, the writer of Hebrews uses the Israelites who followed Moses in the Exodus as an example of what will happen to the early Christians if they allow their belief in Christ to wane. The Israelites received the Ten Commandments. They ate manna from the hand of God. Yet they still hardened their hearts to Yahweh. As the letter states, "Now who were they who heard and yet were rebellious? Was it not all those who left Egypt under the leadership of Moses? . . . And to whom did he swear that they would not enter his rest, if not to those who were disobedient? So we see that they were unable to enter because of unbelief" (Hebrews 3:16, 18-19).

Does the fact that this passage calls for an examination of conscience mean that it is not encouraging? Not in the least! In fact, when we hear words that are meant to console us, if they don't make us pray, read Scripture, repent, or examine our hearts—in other words, if they don't cause us to grow more like Christ—can they really be considered encouragement? Sweet-sounding words might make us feel good for a short time, but in the long run they will not give us what we need to keep running the race and to hold fast to the Lord in faith and trust.

Neither should we gauge encouragement based merely upon how it makes us feel. If a patient has a heart condition, a good doctor doesn't simply console the patient with sympathy! A good doctor will speak truthfully about the prognosis and explain risks for the patient if he should fail to change to a healthier lifestyle.

This passage is not calling for superhuman willpower but for faith in a God whose power transcends our own. The message is that we must put our faith into action. The Israelites were unable to enter the promised land "because of unbelief" (Hebrews 3:19). God has led us out of the desert of unbelief to a life of faith. Let us not allow that spark of life to blow out or grow dim. Instead, let us examine our state before God to ensure that we do not fall by the wayside but heed his words of true encouragement.

"Lord, I want to keep my ears open to your word, and my heart soft to your movements. Father, help me to embrace every word of encouragement you speak to me, even if it means that I must change. Lord, I trust in your love and provision!"

Hebrews 4:1-5

[1] Therefore, while the promise of entering his rest is still open, let us take care that none of you should seem to have failed to reach it. [2]For indeed the good news came to us just as to them; but the message they heard did not benefit them, because they were not united by faith with those who listened. [3]For we who have believed enter that rest, just as God has said,

"As in my anger I swore,

'They shall not enter my rest,'"

though his works were finished at the foundation of the world. [4]For in one place it speaks about the seventh day as follows, "And God rested on the seventh day from all his works." [5]And again in this place it says, "They shall not enter my rest."

The Israelites in the Old Testament were denied their "rest" in the promised land for a whole generation because of their lack of faith. The author of Hebrews warns the early Christians to maintain their faith in God so that they will not be denied the "rest" of their union with Christ. We also could stand to be reminded to put our faith in God so that we will be able to join our Savior in heaven.

But why is it so difficult for us to give our lives to God? The answer, it seems, is that we don't really know how deeply God loves us, because we don't really understand the benefits. If we only knew what awaited us, the costs would seem inconsequential.

For example, if two people contemplating marriage were to stop and enumerate all the costs, they might never proceed with their plans. To begin, there would be the financial cost of the ceremony, the honeymoon, and setting up a new home together. Consider the hassle of raising children; the expense of feeding, clothing, and educating them; the lost freedom. Does all of this frighten young couples into changing their plans? In most cases, no; they overcome these "obstacles" because they love and know they are loved.

When it comes to giving our lives to God, however, we may be tempted to consider the costs insurmountable because they seem higher than our experience of his love. The more we experience Jesus' love, the less intimidating the "cost" will appear. All the problems that loom so large become inconsequential and easily solved as we learn to rely on God's wisdom, revealed in his word and in his church.

Jesus made it clear that there is a price to be paid for living out the gospel, but that there are abundant blessings as well. Let us ask the Spirit of God to strengthen us with a deeper knowledge of his love and power at work within us. As we respond to the Spirit, we can turn from our own ways and come into the rest that God has promised. Let us ask him to soften our hearts lest we fail to reach that rest.

"Jesus, soften my heart so that I may truly experience your love for me. Through the wisdom of your Spirit, help me see that no price is too great to attain the rest you have promised me in heaven."

Hebrews 4:6-11

[6]Since therefore it remains open for some to enter it, and those who formerly received the good news failed to enter because of disobedience, [7]again he sets a certain day—"today"—saying through David much later, in the words already quoted, "Today, if you hear his voice, do not harden your hearts." [8]For if Joshua had given them rest, God would not speak later about another day. [9]So then,

a Sabbath rest still remains for the people of God; [10]for those who enter God's rest also cease from their labors as God did from his. [11]Let us therefore make every effort to enter that rest, so that no one may fall through such disobedience as theirs.

D id you catch the play on words in this passage? "Let us therefore make every effort to enter that rest" (Hebrews 4:11); or transliterated, it might read: let us *work hard* at *resting*." What a clever way to emphasize the unique concept of "rest" that is part of the Christian life!

The renowned preacher St. John Chrysostom (c. 347–407) commented that this "rest" referred to "the kingdom of Heaven." Chrysostom observed:

> That is indeed rest, where "pain, sorrow, and sighing are fled away" (Isaiah 35:10); where there are neither cares, nor labors, nor struggle, nor fear stunning and shaking the soul; but only that fear of God which is full of delight. There is not, "In the sweat of your face you shall eat your bread," nor "thorns and thistles" (Genesis 3:18,19); no longer, "In sorrow shall you bring forth children" (3:16).

By making all these references to the Book of Genesis, Chrysostom hinted that this rest can be considered the removal of the curse that resulted from the fall of our first parents. "Rest" is not just the end of our labor, it is the end of our separation from God. Chrysostom added:

> All is peace, joy, gladness, pleasure, goodness, gentleness. There is no jealousy, nor envy, no sickness, no death

whether of the body, or of the soul. There is no darkness nor night; all is day, all light, all things are bright. It is not possible to be weary, it is not possible to be filled: We shall always persevere in the desire of good things. (*Homilies on the Epistle to the Hebrews*, IV)

Chrysostom saw the "sabbath rest" that "still remains for the people of God" (Hebrews 4:9) as something that our Father in heaven has planned for us from before creation. He saw that it involves something much deeper—and far more fulfilling—than a pleasant nap on a quiet Sunday afternoon.

Although the *fullness* of God's kingdom is still to come, his salvation is present *now*. It broke into human history with Jesus' birth. It broke into our lives when we accepted Jesus into our hearts and welcomed the outpouring of the Holy Spirit. Jesus' salvation is present now as we celebrate the Eucharist with open, humble, and willing hearts.

Walking as God's children can be taxing some days. But what a mistake it would be to stop struggling and laboring to grow in holiness. Let us keep in mind that the reward for our labor is the ultimate rest of union with God.

"Father, I praise you for your marvelous plan of salvation in Christ. You offer us so much more than rest from our weariness. You want to *fill* us with your life and to *enliven* us with your joy. Lord, I will follow you, knowing that in your presence is nothing but pure delight!"

Hebrews 4:12-16

[12] Indeed, the word of God is living and active, sharper than any two-edged sword, piercing until it divides soul from spirit, joints from marrow; it is able to judge the thoughts and intentions of the heart. [13]And before him no creature is hidden, but all are naked and laid bare to the eyes of the one to whom we must render an account.

[14] Since, then, we have a great high priest who has passed through the heavens, Jesus, the Son of God, let us hold fast to our confession. [15]For we do not have a high priest who is unable to sympathize with our weaknesses, but we have one who in every respect has been tested as we are, yet without sin. [16]Let us therefore approach the throne of grace with boldness, so that we may receive mercy and find grace to help in time of need.

The word of God is living and active . . . it is able to judge the thoughts and intentions of the heart. —Hebrews 4:12,13

God sees everything, even our most secret thoughts. Does that scare you? Sometimes we reason that if God were to know what we think, then he would surely be angry. But he's not angry. He does see everything in us; we can't hide from him. Yet, he does not judge us. Instead, he invites us to come before him confident in his unconditional love and forgiveness.

Jesus doesn't want to show us our sins to make us feel bad. He uses our sins as a starting point to reveal his amazing love and mercy. When he had dinner at Levi's house, Jesus was surrounded by sinners. The religious leaders disapproved, but Jesus was doing exactly what he was supposed to do. He was seeking out those who were lost, telling them that they needed to stop sinning and change their ways. But he was doing so in a way that must have softened their hearts and brought them hope.

Jesus wants to expose all that is within us to his light—not to shame us, but to heal us. Imagine what life would be like if you were freed from *everything* that tends to weigh you down. Are you afraid of loving again because of a wounded relationship? Are you racked with guilt, feeling that God could never forgive you for what you've done? Whatever it is, Jesus wants to expose it and take away your fear and pain. He wants to show you he has already forgiven you.

Jesus' words have the power to cut away sin and lift you up to God's grace. He wants to fill you with hope and the love of a personal God. As you read Scripture today, allow the word of God to minister to you. Don't try to hide from your heavenly Father. He doesn't want to condemn you or judge you—he wants to heal you and free you with his immeasurable love.

"Jesus, help me hear your word more clearly, so I can be set free. Help me open myself to the Father's searching gaze so that I can be healed."

Hebrews 5:1-10

[1] Every high priest chosen from among mortals is put in charge of things pertaining to God on their behalf, to offer gifts and sacrifices for sins. [2]He is able to deal gently with the ignorant and wayward, since he himself is subject to weakness; [3]and because of this he must offer sacrifice for his own sins as well as for those of the people. [4]And one does not presume to take this honor, but takes it only when called by God, just as Aaron was.

⁵ So also Christ did not glorify himself in becoming a high priest, but was appointed by the one who said to him,

"You are my Son,

today I have begotten you";

⁶as he says also in another place,

"You are a priest forever,

according to the order of Melchizedek."

⁷ In the days of his flesh, Jesus offered up prayers and supplications, with loud cries and tears, to the one who was able to save him from death, and he was heard because of his reverent submission. ⁸Although he was a Son, he learned obedience through what he suffered; ⁹and having been made perfect, he became the source of eternal salvation for all who obey him, ¹⁰having been designated by God a high priest according to the order of Melchizedek.

After the Israelites' exodus from Egypt, God commanded Moses to consecrate his brother Aaron, of the tribe of Levi, and Aaron's sons as priests (Leviticus 8:1-13). Under Jewish law, a priest's primary role was to mediate between God and his people, offering daily sacrifices and interceding before God on their behalf. Most important, once a year on the Day of Atonement, the high priest—the supreme mediator—was to enter the tent called the Holy of Holies and offer sacrifices for the pardon of Israel's faults (Leviticus 16).

The author of Hebrews points out that the high priest himself was "subject to weakness; and because of this he must offer sacrifice for his own sins as well as for those of the people" (Hebrews 5:3). This is why, according to Hebrews, Jesus surpassed and transcended the priesthood of the Old Testament. Acting as more than a mediator, he offered his own life for us. Jesus himself is the perfect high priest through whom we are sanctified, and the perfect sacrifice who has become the source of our eternal salvation (5:9).

St. John Fisher wrote:

> Our high priest is Christ, our sacrifice is his precious body. . . . Christ first offered sacrifice here on earth, when he underwent his most bitter death. Then, clothed in the new garment of immortality, with his own blood he entered into the Holy of Holies, that is, into heaven. There he also displayed before the throne of the heavenly Father that blood of immeasurable price which he had poured out on behalf of all men subject to sin. (*Commentary on the Psalms*)

Let us rejoice today that we have such a high priest! Though sinless, Jesus knows and understands all our weaknesses and pain. He ever intercedes for us before the throne of God, joining our prayers to his own and bringing them before God (Hebrews 7:25; 9:24).

"Thank you, Jesus, merciful and eternal high priest, for giving your life for me. Thank you for opening the way to the Father through your holy and perfect sacrifice."

Hebrews 5:11-14

[11] About this we have much to say that is hard to explain, since you have become dull in understanding. [12]For though by this time you ought to be teachers, you need someone to teach you again the basic elements of the oracles of God. You need milk, not solid food;

¹³for everyone who lives on milk, being still an infant, is unskilled in the word of righteousness. ¹⁴But solid food is for the mature, for those whose faculties have been trained by practice to distinguish good from evil.

These few, short verses issue a challenge to those of us who may think we are "mature" in our faith (5:14). While of course there are levels of maturity in the Christian life, the author of Hebrews cautions all of us to guard against allowing ourselves to become content with our level of maturity, lest we become "dull in understanding" (5:11).

St. John Vianney, also known as the Curé D'Ars (1786–1859), was revered as a very effective confessor and pastor. He saw the risk for believers to fall into routines that could lead to what he called a "luke-warm soul":

> A lukewarm soul is not yet quite dead in the eyes of God because the faith, the hope, and the charity which are its spiritual life are not altogether extinct. But it is a faith without zeal, a hope without resolution, a charity without ardor. . . .
>
> Nothing touches this soul: It hears the word of God, yes, that is true; but often it just bores it. Its possessor hears it with difficulty, more or less by habit, like someone who thinks that he knows enough about it and does enough of what he should.
>
> In the morning it is not God who occupies his thoughts, nor the salvation of his soul; he is quite taken up with

thoughts of work. His mind is so wrapped up in the things of earth that the thought of God has no place in it.

A lukewarm soul will not, if you like, commit the big sins. But some slander or backbiting, a lie, a feeling of hatred, of dislike, of jealousy, a slight touch of deceit or double-dealing—these count for nothing with it.

The lukewarm soul shuts God up in an obscure and ugly kind of prison. God can find little joy or consolation in his heart. All his dispositions proclaim that his poor soul is struggling for the breath of life.

Alas, my brethren, how many seem to be good Christians in the eyes of the world who are really tepid souls in the eyes of God, who knows our inmost hearts. . . .

Let us ask God with all our hearts, if we are in this state, to give us the grace to get out of it, so that we may take the route that all the saints have taken and arrive at the happiness that they are enjoying. (*The Sermons of the Curé D'Ars*)

"Come, Holy Spirit, and bring your light and fire to my heart. Burn away any dullness. Enlighten any darkness. Melt any coldness. Soften any hardness. Jesus, I want to live only for you!"

Hebrews 6:1-8

[1] Therefore let us go on toward perfection, leaving behind the basic teaching about Christ, and not laying again the foundation: repentance from dead works and faith toward God, [2]instruction about baptisms, laying on of hands, resurrection of the dead, and

eternal judgment. [3]And we will do this, if God permits. [4]For it is impossible to restore again to repentance those who have once been enlightened, and have tasted the heavenly gift, and have shared in the Holy Spirit, [5]and have tasted the goodness of the word of God and the powers of the age to come, [6]and then have fallen away, since on their own they are crucifying again the Son of God and are holding him up to contempt. [7]Ground that drinks up the rain falling on it repeatedly, and that produces a crop useful to those for whom it is cultivated, receives a blessing from God. [8]But if it produces thorns and thistles, it is worthless and on the verge of being cursed; its end is to be burned over.

Therefore, let us go on toward perfection. —Hebrews 6:1

In the exhortation quoted above, the Greek word translated as "perfection" can also be translated as "maturity" or "full growth." Like Jesus' call to be "perfect" as your heavenly Father is "perfect" (Matthew 5:48), it is a call to live up to our full potential, to do everything fully in accord with who we are and what we are meant to become.

Our natural reaction to such a calling is to consider it impossible. Sin is, after all, still very much a part of our experience! Author C.S. Lewis addressed this reaction in his book *Mere Christianity*. Talking about Christian morality and specifically the virtue of chastity, Lewis said we cannot be afraid to return again and again to God for mercy and grace:

> You must ask for God's help. Even when you have done so, it may seem to you for a long time that no help, or less help than you need, is being given. Never mind. After each failure, ask forgiveness, pick yourself up, and try again. Very often

what God first helps us towards is not the virtue itself but just this power of always trying again. For however important chastity (or courage, or truthfulness, or any other virtue) may be, this process trains us in habits of the soul that are more important still. It cures our illusions about ourselves and teaches us to depend on God. We learn, on the one hand, that we cannot trust ourselves even in our best moments, and, on the other, that we need not despair even in our worst, for our failures are forgiven. The only fatal thing is to sit down content with anything less than perfection. (*Mere Christianity*, Book III, Chapter 5)

Perfection means wholeness and completeness. As things stand, we are not whole, because sin has affected us in ways we may not even realize. Still, God's love for us is so great that he won't settle for anything less than making us completely whole again. In Christ, he has called us to himself to restore all of us to the full union with him that he destined for us before we were even born. He even rescued us from sin with the blood of his only Son and poured out the Holy Spirit to transform us. How will he not bring us to "perfection" if we stay close to him?

"O Lord, I accept your call to grow in maturity. I understand that I cannot achieve this perfection on my own. I will continue to walk in faith so that you can bring to completion the good work you began in me. I praise you, Lord, for wanting nothing but the best for my life."

Hebrews 6:9-12

[9] Even though we speak in this way, beloved, we are confident of better things in your case, things that belong to salvation. [10]For God is not unjust; he will not overlook your work and the love that you showed for his sake in serving the saints, as you still do. [11]And we want each one of you to show the same diligence so as to realize the full assurance of hope to the very end, [12]so that you may not become sluggish, but imitators of those who through faith and patience inherit the promises.

Our God loves us dearly and is infinitely patient with us. In him, justice and kindness meet—to our benefit (Psalm 85:10-11). Often, he looks on us more kindly than we do ourselves. We sometimes find it hard to believe that God delights in pouring out love on anyone who is open to receiving it. But God is on our side. He has no book of black marks against us. Nothing is hidden from him. He sees everything we do—the wrongs, yes, but also the good we do. "For God is not unjust; he will not overlook your work and the love that you showed for his sake in serving the saints, as you still do" (Hebrews 6:10).

Here, as elsewhere in the New Testament, "saints" refers to the people of God in general—to everyone who has been set apart for the Lord through faith and baptism. We are the saints. Our fathers and mothers, sisters and brothers are the saints. Our children are the saints. The people we sit next to at Mass are the saints. How often do we think of all these people as saints—and think of the routine ways that we care for them as "serving the saints" (Hebrews 6:10)? And yet, that is what they are.

Raising children, teaching in a religious education program, seating latecomers to Mass—none of these works goes unheeded by God. Nor is any of this supposed to depend solely on our abilities, without his help. No! God sees us. He knows our service and is always ready to pour out his grace on us.

So, let's not lose heart! God sees our work. Indeed, he himself urges us to accomplish it. We have reason to rejoice, for God is pleased by the smallest kindness we do in his name. He will bless us as we care for others and try to bring the gospel to them. He does not wait for us to get everything just right before he gives his blessing. Rather, he looks at our hearts. He is near to us (Psalm 145:18). He wants to show his love to others through us. Let's be among those "who through faith and patience inherit the promises" (Hebrews 6:12).

"Father, bless all who serve the gospel in any way. Shower your love on them. Prosper their efforts to proclaim the truth. Fill them with hope in you!"

Hebrews 6:13-20

[13] When God made a promise to Abraham, because he had no one greater by whom to swear, he swore by himself, [14]saying, "I will surely bless you and multiply you."[15] And thus Abraham, having patiently endured, obtained the promise. [16]Human beings, of course, swear by someone greater than themselves, and an oath given as confirmation puts an end to all dispute. [17]In the same way, when God desired to show even more clearly to the heirs of the promise the unchangeable character of his purpose, he guaranteed it by an oath, [18]so that through two unchangeable things, in which

it is impossible that God would prove false, we who have taken refuge might be strongly encouraged to seize the hope set before us. [19]We have this hope, a sure and steadfast anchor of the soul, a hope that enters the inner shrine behind the curtain, [20]where Jesus, a forerunner on our behalf, has entered, having become a high priest forever according to the order of Melchizedek.

L
ike the early Christians who first heard this sermon, we too are often in need of an exhortation to persevere in our daily walk with Jesus. How easily we can become discouraged and want to give up! How easily we can become overconfident and proud, separating ourselves from the presence of the Lord! If we want to reach our goal, we need determination, conviction, and vigor. Yet these can seem impossible to maintain on a day-to-day basis. We may wonder, at times, if we will ever cross the finish line intact!

Throughout our days, the Holy Spirit wants to remind us that we have a sure and steadfast anchor for our souls. By paying the price for our sins, Jesus has removed the veil that separated us from God. As our forerunner, now seated in heaven, Jesus has promised to intercede for us and to be with us always. He is ever faithful to the covenant he made with us (see Psalm 111:4-5). What strength we can gain from this truth when we find ourselves doubting!

Scripture is brimming with stories of people who, by their faith in God, accomplished what was humanly impossible. Recall the story of Abraham, who although he was old and didn't have an heir, was promised by God to have descendants as numerous as the stars (Genesis 15:5). For almost twenty-five years, Abraham trusted God. He believed, and he finally saw the promise fulfilled! As Abraham's descendants by faith, we have no less reason to believe that God will bring to completion all of his promises to us.

While our fallen condition can lead us to doubt God's word and sometimes choose not to obey him, God remains our refuge. He is always ready to forgive and heal those who turn to him. Our hope rests in Jesus' sacrifice. He has secured for us an eternal salvation. Let us "seize the hope set before us" (Hebrews 6:18). Nothing can stand against us when we are rooted in Christ. We can have great confidence in God. Let this knowledge guide you and keep you confidently anchored in Jesus, the fulfillment of all God's promises.

"Lord Jesus, I abandon myself to you and your will for me. Grant me faith and patience that I too may persevere to the end and come to inherit your promises."

Hebrews 7:1-14

[1] This "King Melchizedek of Salem, priest of the Most High God, met Abraham as he was returning from defeating the kings and blessed him"; [2]and to him Abraham apportioned "one-tenth of everything." His name, in the first place, means "king of righteousness"; next he is also king of Salem, that is, "king of peace." [3]Without father, without mother, without genealogy, having neither beginning of days nor end of life, but resembling the Son of God, he remains a priest forever.

[4] See how great he is! Even Abraham the patriarch gave him a tenth of the spoils. [5]And those descendants of Levi who receive the priestly office have a commandment in the law to collect tithes from the people, that is, from their kindred, though these also are descended from Abraham. [6]But this man, who does not belong to

their ancestry, collected tithes from Abraham and blessed him who had received the promises. [7]It is beyond dispute that the inferior is blessed by the superior. [8]In the one case, tithes are received by those who are mortal; in the other, by one of whom it is testified that he lives. [9]One might even say that Levi himself, who receives tithes, paid tithes through Abraham, [10]for he was still in the loins of his ancestor when Melchizedek met him.

[11] Now if perfection had been attainable through the Levitical priesthood—for the people received the law under this priesthood—what further need would there have been to speak of another priest arising according to the order of Melchizedek, rather than one according to the order of Aaron? [12]For when there is a change in the priesthood, there is necessarily a change in the law as well. [13]Now the one of whom these things are spoken belonged to another tribe, from which no one has ever served at the altar. [14]For it is evident that our Lord was descended from Judah, and in connection with that tribe Moses said nothing about priests.

Melchizedek was the priest who blessed Abraham when Abraham returned from defeating King Chedorlaomer of Elam (Genesis 14:17). In Jewish law, the office of the priesthood was reserved for those from Levi's line, from the family of Aaron. Once ordained, a priest remained in office until he died. Melchizedek's priesthood, however, was distinct from this pattern in two ways: He was not descended from the line of Levi (who hadn't even been born yet), and it was said that he never died.

How could this be? According to rabbinic tradition, whatever is not mentioned in the Torah (the first five books of the Bible) did not exist.

There is no mention in the Torah of Melchizedek's ancestry, birth, or death. Based on this tradition, one would have to conclude that Melchizedek's priesthood was eternal and had been granted directly from God. Thus his priesthood would be better, or higher, than the Levitical priesthood. "Without father, without mother, without genealogy, having neither beginning of days nor end of life, but resembling the Son of God, he remains a priest forever" (Hebrews 7:3).

The Jews were familiar with the tradition regarding Melchizedek, and the writer of Hebrews used it to illustrate the greatness of Jesus' priesthood. Like Melchizedek, Jesus became a priest "not through a legal requirement concerning physical descent, but through the power of an indestructible life" (Hebrews 7:16). Jesus did not come from the family line of Aaron even in his earthly lineage; he descended form his throne in heaven. After he had made perfect atonement for our sins by shedding his blood on the cross, he returned to his throne to reign as king and high priest forever.

Levitical high priests shared in the sins of the people, and so they could not make peace with God once and for all. They could not offer a perfect sacrifice to God once and for all. Jesus is the greater high priest because he shed his own sinless blood, offering himself as the perfect sacrifice to God for all of our sins for all time.

"Lord Jesus, you are the eternal high priest who has made atonement for our sins. Your priesthood did what the Levitical priesthood never could do: It gave us the chance for eternal life. We give you our lives in love to serve you and your church."

Hebrews 7:15-22

[15] It is even more obvious when another priest arises, resembling Melchizedek, [16]one who has become a priest, not through a legal requirement concerning physical descent, but through the power of an indestructible life. [17]For it is attested of him,

"You are a priest forever,
according to the order of Melchizedek."

[18]There is, on the one hand, the abrogation of an earlier commandment because it was weak and ineffectual [19](for the law made nothing perfect); there is, on the other hand, the introduction of a better hope, through which we approach God.

[20] This was confirmed with an oath; for others who became priests took their office without an oath, [21]but this one became a priest with an oath, because of the one who said to him,

"The Lord has sworn
and will not change his mind,
'You are a priest forever'"—

[22]accordingly Jesus has also become the guarantee of a better covenant.

What a progression! First, the author of Hebrews said that Jesus is superior over the angels (Hebrews 1:4–2:18). Then, he spoke of Jesus' superiority over Moses (3:1–4:13). And now, he states that Jesus surpasses all of the Levitical priests, and even Melchizedek himself, the ideal, perfect priest. Why such superiority? Because Jesus' ministry came not as a result of "physical descent" but "through the power of an indestructible life" (7:16-17).

With so much superiority surrounding Jesus, it's no wonder that the author proclaimed that in Christ we all have a "better hope" (Hebrews 7:19). But at the same time, he issued a challenge to his readers. They had to examine long-held beliefs, old habits, and a perhaps too-comfortable reliance on the law. They had to do more than simply say, "Jesus is Lord." They had to put their faith in the better hope of the new covenant in Christ.

The challenge holds true for us, too. It's only natural to want a better job, a trouble-free marriage, a nicer home, lots of friends, happy children, good health, and so much more. But are there times when the things of this world become all that we hope for? If so, we could fall into a trap: What if we do not get that raise, obtain that house, or find the perfect spouse? What if we must struggle with loneliness or family problems? Do we lose our faith in God then?

Of course, it isn't wrong to try to better ourselves, our families, or our careers. It's wise to plan and be responsible stewards in all our affairs. But if our hope lies solely in reaching a better place in the world, we really are no different from nonbelievers.

Consider the witness of Mother Teresa of Calcutta. She was already in a religious order when she felt called by God to do more. It must have caused great upheaval to leave her friends and family for a whole new place and an entirely different ministry. In beginning to reach out to the poorest of the poor, her burdens must have multiplied exponentially! She had to arrange shelter for an increasing number of people, find food and medicine for them, and train others in her unique way of service. But in the midst of all these burdens, Mother Teresa placed her hope in following Christ, not in finding a conventional, comfortable life with no problems or worries. And the world is better off because of her obedience—just as it will be when we place all our hope in Christ.

"O Jesus, you are superior to all things in this world. Teach me to place my hope in you above all else."

Hebrews 7:23–8:5

23 Furthermore, the former priests were many in number, because they were prevented by death from continuing in office; 24but he holds his priesthood permanently, because he continues forever. 25Consequently he is able for all time to save those who approach God through him, since he always lives to make intercession for them.

26 For it was fitting that we should have such a high priest, holy, blameless, undefiled, separated from sinners, and exalted above the heavens. 27Unlike the other high priests, he has no need to offer sacrifices day after day, first for his own sins, and then for those of the people; this he did once for all when he offered himself. 28For the law appoints as high priests those who are subject to weakness, but the word of the oath, which came later than the law, appoints a Son who has been made perfect forever.

1 Now the main point in what we are saying is this: we have such a high priest, one who is seated at the right hand of the throne of the Majesty in the heavens, 2a minister in the sanctuary and the true tent that the Lord, and not any mortal, has set up. 3For every high priest is appointed to offer gifts and sacrifices; hence it is necessary for this priest also to have something to offer. 4Now if he were on earth, he would not be a priest at all, since there are priests who offer gifts according to the law. 5They offer worship in a sanctuary that is a sketch and shadow of the heavenly one; for Moses,

when he was about to erect the tent, was warned, "See that you make everything according to the pattern that was shown you on the mountain."

Consequently he is able for all time to save those who approach God through him, since he always lives to make intercession for them.
—Hebrews 7:25

Can you imagine the scene? Jesus, our great high priest, is always in the presence of God, interceding for us. And if the one who is "holy, blameless, undefiled, separated from sinners"—in other words, perfect—is interceding for us, then his intercession must be perfect (Hebrews 7:26). This should give us great hope!

Jesus knows what we need, and so we can easily join our prayers with his and know that they will be heard (Hebrews 4:15-16). This means that we can come boldly into the presence of God and pray with great confidence. Scripture also promises that if we remain in Jesus, and if we allow his words to remain in us, then we can ask for whatever we please, and he will answer us (John 15:7). This is not because we have earned God's favor, but simply because we belong to Christ, and his sacrifice has made perfect atonement for our sin.

We don't have to settle for vague, weak prayers of intercession, fearing that if we are too specific, God might not listen to us. Because we have the confidence that Jesus is interceding for us and with us, we can dare to be specific. As we join our wills with the will of the one who loves us and gave his life for us, we never have to fear bringing our needs before our loving Father.

As you experiment with intercession, don't be surprised to find God leading your prayer. He might, for example, move you to pray for the healing of a relative with a serious illness, for a spouse to receive a job promotion, or for a friend to be freed from bondage to fear. Whatever your needs or desires, go boldly to your heavenly Father, confident that he will supply all of your needs (Philippians 4:19). Seek to pray in union with Jesus, the perfect one, and you can trust that he will make perfect intercession with you.

"Thank you, Jesus, for being my great high priest. Thank you that you live forever to intercede for me. I place my trust and hope in you, and I believe that you know what I need better than I do myself."

Hebrews 8:6-13

[6] But Jesus has now obtained a more excellent ministry, and to that degree he is the mediator of a better covenant, which has been enacted through better promises. [7]For if that first covenant had been faultless, there would have been no need to look for a second one.

[8] God finds fault with them when he says:
"The days are surely coming, says the Lord,
> when I will establish a new covenant with the house of Israel
> and with the house of Judah;
[9] not like the covenant that I made with their ancestors,
> on the day when I took them by the hand to lead them
> out of the land of Egypt;
for they did not continue in my covenant,
> and so I had no concern for them, says the Lord.
[10] This is the covenant that I will make with the house of Israel
> after those days, says the Lord:
I will put my laws in their minds,

and write them on their hearts,
and I will be their God,
and they shall be my people.

11 And they shall not teach one another
or say to each other, 'Know the Lord,'
for they shall all know me,
from the least of them to the greatest.

12 For I will be merciful toward their iniquities,
and I will remember their sins no more."

13In speaking of "a new covenant," he has made the first one obsolete. And what is obsolete and growing old will soon disappear.

The author of Hebrews, writing to a community of Jewish Christians in the first century, tried to make clear for his readers the new reality that they had begun to experience. As Jews who had come to believe in Jesus the Messiah, they had entered a new era. The repeated sacrifices required under the Mosaic covenant now held only a symbolic meaning for them. The author explained that the new covenant through Jesus is radically better than the relationship with God granted through the Mosaic covenant. "But Jesus has now obtained a more excellent ministry, and to that degree he is the mediator of a better covenant, which has been enacted through better promises" (Hebrews 8:6).

The old covenant instructed people in the right way to live, but it didn't transform their minds and hearts. As good and necessary as the law was, it could not bring with it the power to carry out its demands. As we well know, we all experience strong tendencies to sin, and this is precisely where the blessing of God's "better promise" lies: "I will put my laws in their minds, and write them on their hearts" (Hebrews

8:10). Through Jesus' sacrifice on the cross, God opened up a deeper access to himself. Now everyone who believes in him has personal access to the Father, where we can receive the power we need to fulfill God's purposes.

Still, we sometimes find it easier to carry out the minimum requirements of the law while keeping God at arm's length. We conform our outward behavior to a set of rules, but close ourselves off to God's love. We settle for being "nice people," or "good citizens," but miss out on the power of the new covenant. As followers of Christ, we should settle for nothing less than everything his death and resurrection have won for us! God longs to give each of us a personal knowledge of himself—a knowledge that will give us a deep desire to live in his ways. Don't settle for a partial gospel! Take hold of God's promises:

> This is the covenant that I will make with the house of Israel after those days, says the Lord: I will put my laws in their minds, and write them on their hearts, and I will be their God, and they shall be my people. And they shall not teach one another or say to each other, 'Know the Lord,' for they shall all know me, from the least of them to the greatest. For I will be merciful toward their iniquities, and I will remember their sins no more. (Hebrews 8:10-12)

Accept his gift of new life. Let these promises transform your prayer, and you will begin to experience their fulfillment in your daily life.

"Thank you, Jesus, for making a new covenant with me. I open my heart to you."

Hebrews 9:1-10

1   Now even the first covenant had regulations for worship and an earthly sanctuary. ²For a tent was constructed, the first one, in which were the lampstand, the table, and the bread of the Presence; this is called the Holy Place. ³Behind the second curtain was a tent called the Holy of Holies. ⁴In it stood the golden altar of incense and the ark of the covenant overlaid on all sides with gold, in which there were a golden urn holding the manna, and Aaron's rod that budded, and the tablets of the covenant; ⁵above it were the cherubim of glory overshadowing the mercy seat. Of these things we cannot speak now in detail.

6   Such preparations having been made, the priests go continually into the first tent to carry out their ritual duties; ⁷but only the high priest goes into the second, and he but once a year, and not without taking the blood that he offers for himself and for the sins committed unintentionally by the people. ⁸By this the Holy Spirit indicates that the way into the sanctuary has not yet been disclosed as long as the first tent is still standing. ⁹This is a symbol of the present time, during which gifts and sacrifices are offered that cannot perfect the conscience of the worshiper, ¹⁰but deal only with food and drink and various baptisms, regulations for the body imposed until the time comes to set things right.

This entire passage is a prelude to Verse 11, which begins, "But when Christ came." And *when* Christ came, everything changed!

The contrast is striking. The beautiful and precise rituals prescribed in the law were designed to keep people from getting too close to the terrifying power of the Holy One. The new way of worship made possible by Jesus' sacrifice is designed to plunge us into the very life of God.

The Jewish temple is here described as dazzling, a powerful symbol of the glory of God. Like our great cathedrals, it enabled the Hebrews to leave behind the cares of their everyday lives and lift their minds and hearts to God. However, the Old Testament tells of sinners who experienced death when they dared to draw too near to that holiness. They sought forgiveness for their sins, but only through a ritual that kept them at a safe distance.

By contrast, a Christian place of worship may be "only a house, the earth its floor, walls and a roof, sheltering people, windows for light, an open door" (from the hymn "What Is This Place?"). Rather than leaving our ordinary lives outside, we bring them to the altar to be transformed, and we ourselves become what we receive, the body of Christ, "the fullness of him who fills all in all" (Ephesians 1:23).

The ark of the covenant contained relics from God's historic acts on behalf of his people: a piece of manna and the rod Moses and Aaron used to perform miracles. The tabernacle in the Christian church contains the living presence of Christ today, available to nourish the people of God. We come together in God's house not just to hear stories about what God did in the past but to share how God is working in our lives and to receive divine strength, spiritual guidance, and brotherly companionship for building his kingdom in our world today.

Trembling, the high priest cleansed himself and entered the Holy of Holies once a year bearing the lifeblood of animals, only to obtain forgiveness for inadvertent violations of the law. But we confess our deliberate sins against God's generosity, and receive his lifeblood poured out to forgive us and make us new.

How reflectively do we make use of the carefully crafted forms and rituals of Christian worship? When we genuflect, bow our heads, make the sign of the cross, express sorrow for sins, and say "Amen," do we do these things in a way that further distances us from the Holy One, or in a way that helps us enter into the divine life God is offering us?

"Father of our Lord Jesus Christ, how great a salvation you have won for us! Help me never to take your great mercy for granted."

Hebrews 9:11-14

[11] But when Christ came as a high priest of the good things that have come, then through the greater and perfect tent (not made with hands, that is, not of this creation), [12]he entered once for all into the Holy Place, not with the blood of goats and calves, but with his own blood, thus obtaining eternal redemption. [13]For if the blood of goats and bulls, with the sprinkling of the ashes of a heifer, sanctifies those who have been defiled so that their flesh is purified, [14]how much more will the blood of Christ, who through the eternal Spirit offered himself without blemish to God, purify our conscience from dead works to worship the living God!

At the heart of the new covenant stands this truth: Jesus' death on the cross does away with sin once and for all. Our consciences—the deepest expression of who we are—can now be cleansed by the perfect, everlasting sacrifice of Jesus. Not some, but *all* sins are abolished. Our consciences aren't merely relieved, they are actually cleansed. This is a crucial truth for us to grasp and believe.

The old covenant provided regulations aimed at relieving the people's consciences, but it had no power to reach in and change the human heart. This is equally true today. Scrupulous observances of regulations may render us legally righteous and outwardly good. But we were created to resemble God, to be filled with divine life and love. This is something that regulations and ceremonies can never accomplish (Hebrews 7:18-19). Merely following rules cannot demolish the hold that envy, anger, shame, or covetousness has on the human heart. Neither can obedience purify our consciences from the stain of guilt that can haunt us so deeply.

Only the blood of Jesus can purify us deep within. How deeply does it penetrate? It penetrates even to dividing "soul from spirit . . . joints from marrow" (Hebrews 4:12). Jesus' blood bathes the very core of our beings. It has the power to redirect our hearts and minds. Persistent habits of sin can be cut off and replaced by new, peace-filled ways of living. Lifelong guilt—that record of sins that replays vividly in our minds—is erased so that we can live in freedom. Wells of misery are drained and refilled with joy.

This is not something we simply hope for. It is reality. It is ours for the asking. Come to Jesus for cleansing. Confess your needs unafraid! It is because of our needs—and Jesus knows each and every one of them—that he shed his blood on the cross. Surrender your heart to Jesus, whose sacrifice of his own life has the power to purify the deepest regions of your heart.

"Lord Jesus, I thank you for dying for me. I thank you for pouring out your blood so that I might be made pleasing in your sight and freed to receive your tender love. Jesus, I am so grateful—I give you my heart to do with as you please."

Hebrews 9:15-23

[15] For this reason he is the mediator of a new covenant, so that those who are called may receive the promised eternal inheritance, because a death has occurred that redeems them from the transgressions under the first covenant. [16]Where a will is involved, the death of the one who made it must be established. [17]For a will takes effect only at death, since it is not in force as long as the one who made it is alive. [18]Hence not even the first covenant was inaugurated without blood. [19]For when every commandment had been told to all the people by Moses in accordance with the law, he took the blood of calves and goats, with water and scarlet wool and hyssop, and sprinkled both the scroll itself and all the people, [20]saying, "This is the blood of the covenant that God has ordained for you." [21]And in the same way he sprinkled with the blood both the tent and all the vessels used in worship. [22]Indeed, under the law almost everything is purified with blood, and without the shedding of blood there is no forgiveness of sins. [23] Thus it was necessary for the sketches of the heavenly things to be purified with these rites, but the heavenly things themselves need better sacrifices than these.

But you promised! Every parent has heard this wail from a disappointed child. Broken promises undermine trust and make it harder for someone to move forward with hope. By contrast, our heavenly Father never breaks a promise. "For the Son of God, Jesus Christ, whom we proclaimed among you . . . was not 'Yes and No'; but in him it is always 'Yes.' For in him every one of God's promises is a 'Yes'" (2 Corinthians 1:19-20). Through Jesus, the Father fulfills his promises to us with a new covenant.

But what's so new about the new covenant in Christ? For one thing, its *effectiveness*.

Sacrifices of animals under the old covenant couldn't effectively conquer sin and death but had to be repeated again and again. But Jesus' death on the cross was the perfect sacrifice that abolishes sin now and forever so that no additional sacrifice needs to be made. As the author of Hebrews puts it, Christ established a new covenant "so that those who are called may receive the promised eternal inheritance" (Hebrews 9:15).

What's new about the new covenant in Christ? Its *extent*.

What Jesus offers is not just a portion of his estate, but all of it. By the death of our Savior, each of us inherits the fullness of God's life: transforming forgiveness, a heart big enough to love without counting the cost, the ability to see God at work and to cooperate with him.

What's new about the new covenant in Christ? Its *expense*.

What child would insist on receiving a promised gift at the cost of a parent's life? Would a child expect his father to step in front of a speeding train to retrieve a rare coin? Think how many of us have urged aging parents to enjoy their resources while they can, rather than hoarding them to pass along to their children.

And yet the writer of Hebrews reminds us that we are redeemed only because Jesus willingly poured out his own lifeblood for us. The testator's death has released all his assets and made them ours.

Moses ratified the old covenant by sprinkling the same blood on the people that he had poured onto the altar of sacrifice. This gesture acted as a temporary reminder of the people's obligations and of God's offer to meet them more than halfway. The blood of Christ, however, is our *permanent* possession. It runs in our veins constantly to cleanse us, heal us, and energize us for Christ-living.

"Lord Jesus, you have sealed your extravagant promises with your lifeblood. Rise up within me and enable me to keep the promises I make in humble gratitude."

Hebrews 9:24-28

[24]For Christ did not enter a sanctuary made by human hands, a mere copy of the true one, but he entered into heaven itself, now to appear in the presence of God on our behalf. [25]Nor was it to offer himself again and again, as the high priest enters the Holy Place year after year with blood that is not his own; [26]for then he would have had to suffer again and again since the foundation of the world. But as it is, he has appeared once for all at the end of the age to remove sin by the sacrifice of himself. [27]And just as it is appointed for mortals to die once, and after that the judgment, [28]so Christ, having been offered once to bear the sins of many, will appear a second time, not to deal with sin, but to save those who are eagerly waiting for him.

Modern western culture seems to hunger for change—for whatever is "new" and "in vogue." It seems commonplace these days to tire of the demands of love and marriage as readily as we exchange our cars and houses. Clothes, computers—even job skills—can become obsolete in a matter of months. Things change so fast that we may be tempted to ask, "Is anything permanent?"

The author of Hebrews had a vision of something truly enduring: the salvation that Jesus won for us. "He has appeared *once for all* at the end of the age to remove sin by the sacrifice of himself" (Hebrews 9:26). Only the Son of God could atone for our sin in such a lasting way. As our great high priest, Jesus was far superior to the priesthood and the sacrifices offered under the old covenant. Unlike those priests, he did not have to make another sin offering day after day, either for himself or for us. "This he did once for all when he offered himself" (Hebrews 7:27). After the cross, it was completed; nothing else was necessary (John 19:30). Because of the cross, we are set free!

Jesus' sacrifice surpassed even the greatness of the Jewish feast of Yom Kippur, the Day of Atonement. On that feast, which was celebrated only once a year, the high priest entered the holiest place in the temple, confessed Israel's sins before God's throne, and sprinkled the altar with the blood of a sacrificial animal. Now, in his death, Jesus forever altered how we relate to God. He "entered into heaven itself" (Hebrews 9:24), the eternal throne of God. And he didn't take "the blood of goats and calves but his own blood, thus securing an eternal redemption" (9:12).

The greatness of such a sacrifice should fill us with confidence and hope. God will never abandon us. No sin is too big for him to forgive. No fear is too strong for him to soothe. No obstacle is too great for him to overcome. Jesus is risen far above all darkness. In faith, let us follow where he has gone.

"Lord Jesus, help us to be generous receivers of your transforming love. By your Spirit, give us the confidence to look forward to the day when you return, 'not to deal with sin, but to save those who are eagerly waiting' for you" (Hebrews 9:28).

Hebrews 10:1-10

[1] Since the law has only a shadow of the good things to come and not the true form of these realities, it can never, by the same sacrifices that are continually offered year after year, make perfect those who approach. [2]Otherwise, would they not have ceased being offered, since the worshipers, cleansed once for all, would no longer

have any consciousness of sin? ³But in these sacrifices there is a reminder of sin year after year. ⁴For it is impossible for the blood of bulls and goats to take away sins. ⁵Consequently, when Christ came into the world, he said,

> "Sacrifices and offerings you have not desired,
>> but a body you have prepared for me;
> 6   in burnt offerings and sin offerings
>> you have taken no pleasure.
> 7   Then I said, 'See, God, I have come to do your will, O God'
>> (in the scroll of the book it is written of me)."

⁸When he said above, "You have neither desired nor taken pleasure in sacrifices and offerings and burnt offerings and sin offerings" (these are offered according to the law), ⁹then he added, "See, I have come to do your will." He abolishes the first in order to establish the second. ¹⁰And it is by God's will that we have been sanctified through the offering of the body of Jesus Christ once for all.

The Mosaic law was a "shadow of the good things to come" (Hebrews 10:1). The sacrifices and offerings of animal blood that were prescribed under the old covenant needed to be performed year after year because they dealt only with ritual uncleanness; they could never fully remove sin from the heart (9:13-14). Only Jesus' sacrifice of his unblemished blood could work such a mighty restoration and healing.

Because of his perfect obedience to the Father, Jesus was able to fulfill the law's just demands and so win our redemption. He loved the Father—and us—so much that he willingly made such a sacrifice. Now, the "sacrifices and offerings" (Hebrews 10:5) of the old covenant have found their fulfillment in the pure disposition of Jesus' heart. There is no more need for all the rituals of expiation and atonement in the old law. We are set free, and God's law of love is now written on our hearts.

Before Jesus even entered into human history, Yahweh had taught his people that burnt sacrifices and offerings were ineffective if they did not arise out of a humble heart open to God. Through the prophet Isaiah, God told his people that "bringing offerings is futile" (Isaiah 1:13). Instead, they were to "cease to do evil, learn to do good" (1:16-17). Similarly, Psalm 51 proclaims, "For you have no delight in sacrifice; if I were to give a burnt offering, you would not be pleased. The sacrifice acceptable to God is a broken spirit; a broken and contrite heart, O God, you will not despise" (Psalm 51:16-17).

In Jesus Christ, the old and new covenants come together and find their fulfillment. The two elements are inseparably linked, and we can receive the grace of both of them as we celebrate the Eucharist together. As we surrender ourselves to the Lord, opening our hearts to him during the liturgy, we will find ourselves moved to obey his commands. Similarly, as we obey his word with humble hearts, we will find our celebration of the Eucharist that much more powerful and effective in bringing us closer to the Lord.

"Fill us with your love, Lord, so that we may approach our Father with humble hearts and pray as you did: 'I have come to do your will, O God' (Hebrews 10:7)."

Hebrews 10:11-18

[11] And every priest stands day after day at his service, offering again and again the same sacrifices that can never take away sins.

[12]But when Christ had offered for all time a single sacrifice for sins, "he sat down at the right hand of God," [13]and since then has been waiting "until his enemies would be made a footstool for his feet." [14]For by a single offering he has perfected for all time those who are sanctified. [15]And the Holy Spirit also testifies to us, for after saying,

[16]   "This is the covenant that I will make with them
         after those days, says the Lord:
     I will put my laws in their hearts,
         and I will write them on their minds,"
[17]he also adds,

     "I will remember their sins and their lawless deeds no more."
[18]Where there is forgiveness of these, there is no longer any offering for sin.

Throughout the Letter to the Hebrews, we read how God has forgiven all our sins through the sacrifice of Jesus on the cross. His blood washed away our sins and the sins of the whole world. What a powerful gift we have received! How freeing it is! We do not have to labor under guilt or strive on our own to be perfect. By his self-offering, Jesus "has perfected for all time those who are sanctified" (Hebrews 10:14).

The forgiveness God has shown us leads to another important type of forgiveness: our forgiveness of others. Experience tells us that forgiving can be very hard to do, especially if someone has hurt us deeply. Yet Jesus places a high priority on our willingness to forgive. He taught us to pray, "forgive us our sins, for we ourselves forgive everyone indebted to us" (Luke 11:4), and that we should forgive "seventy-seven times" (Matthew 18:22).

Just as God's forgiveness brings us freedom, so too in a lesser but important way does our forgiveness bring freedom to those who have wronged us. Jesus told his disciples, "If you forgive the sins of any, they are forgiven them; if you retain the sins of any, they are retained" (John 20:23). Of course, the fullness of forgiveness (and hence, salvation) is only God's to give. Nevertheless, there is a way that we can hold people in a kind of bondage when we withhold forgiveness.

We ourselves have enjoyed the experience of being forgiven for the wrongs we have committed. Let us share this experience with others by forgiving them. As we do, those who have sinned against us are released from the burden of our hatred or judgment and are freer to open their hearts to God's mercy.

God has invited us to share in his ministry of reconciliation (2 Corinthians 5:18). Is there someone who needs your forgiveness? A relationship that needs healing? Ask the Holy Spirit to help you forgive as Jesus did. Your forgiveness can be life-giving—for you as well as for the one you are forgiving!

"Father, help me forgive those who have sinned against me, just as completely as you have forgiven me. Holy Spirit, help me to be merciful with the mercy of Jesus."

Hebrews 10:19-25

[19] Therefore, my friends, since we have confidence to enter the sanctuary by the blood of Jesus, [20]by the new and living way that he opened for us through the curtain (that is, through his flesh), [21]and since we have a great priest over the house of God, [22]let us approach with a true heart in full assurance of faith, with our hearts

sprinkled clean from an evil conscience and our bodies washed with pure water. [23]Let us hold fast to the confession of our hope without wavering, for he who has promised is faithful. [24]And let us consider how to provoke one another to love and good deeds, [25]not neglecting to meet together, as is the habit of some, but encouraging one another, and all the more as you see the Day approaching.

T he Letter to the Hebrews proclaims that we can come into God's presence because Jesus' death and resurrection have removed the barriers that had previously separated us. What is the basis of such a bold assertion?

The basis rests on faith in the power of God. Because Jesus has removed the sin and guilt that prevented us from knowing God's love—because he has broken the power of Satan that prevented us from *yielding* to that love—we can decide in faith to draw near to God every day, through our prayer, at the Eucharist, and as we serve one another.

Even in times of trouble, worry, or failure, we can come to God full of hope. Our hope is not based on our having done everything right, but on God's faithfulness to his promises, the greatest of which is the promise of redemption by his beloved Son. Through Jesus' passion, death, and resurrection, our sin is forgiven; our consciences are cleansed from the "dead works" of the old life we inherited from Adam (Hebrews 9:14). Jesus' blood has brought us, who were formerly far away, near to God. (Ephesians 2:13). It has opened a new way of life for us (Hebrews 10:20) and has the power to make us holy (13:12). Not only does Jesus' blood cleanse us from all sin (1 John 1:7), it enables us to overcome the temptations of "the accuser" (Revelation 12:10-11).

What wonderful news! We can take all our burdens, failures, and anxieties to Jesus. He loves us and is very close to us in our times of need. Because he has opened the way for us through his blood, we can approach God any time, any place, whatever the circumstance. By faith, through hope, and in love, we will receive all that we need.

"Jesus, we come to you with our great burdens. According to your great love, cleanse us, forgive us, and remove our guilt. Out of your abundant mercy, draw us near to you. From our position of weakness, doubt, and caution, give us courage, confidence, and boldness. Strengthened by your Spirit, help us to encourage others in their faith as well."

Hebrews 10:26-31

26 For if we willfully persist in sin after having received the knowledge of the truth, there no longer remains a sacrifice for sins, 27but a fearful prospect of judgment, and a fury of fire that will consume the adversaries. 28Anyone who has violated the law of Moses dies without mercy "on the testimony of two or three witnesses." 29How much worse punishment do you think will be deserved by those who have spurned the Son of God, profaned the blood of the covenant by which they were sanctified, and outraged the Spirit of grace? 30For we know the one who said, "Vengeance is mine, I will repay." And again, "The Lord will judge his people." 31It is a fearful thing to fall into the hands of the living God.

A fearful prospect of judgment, and a fury of fire. . . .
much worse punishment . . . deserved by those who have . . .
outraged the spirit of grace . . .
Vengeance is mine, I will repay. . . .
It is a fearful thing to fall into the hands of the living God.
—Hebrews 10:27-31

What an ominous passage! How can these words follow so closely on the admonition to encourage one another all the more as you see the day approaching (Hebrews 10:25)?

Although the author of Hebrews has spoken repeatedly about what our salvation cost the Son of God, he wants to make sure that the reader doesn't overlook the seriousness of the sin from which we have been saved. His biggest concern is that we not "willfully persist in sin after having received the knowledge of the truth" (10:26). And so he is convinced that only if we see the sinkhole of sin can we begin to understand the ocean depth of God's love and mercy.

What is sin? It means "spurn[ing] the Son of God" (Hebrews 10:29), turning our back on the Savior in the mistaken notion that we can earn salvation by ourselves. It means "profaning the blood of the covenant" by which we were "sanctified," considering ourselves outside God's people and unworthy of forgiveness. It means "outrag[ing] the spirit of grace," as if God couldn't muster up the grace or power to deliver us from evil, whether internal or external.

What does God consider "outrageous"? Not our most heinous sin; surely he's seen it all before! What is outrageous is acting as if we can save ourselves—and then giving up hope when we find that task impossible!

In this fallen world, sin is inevitable. But our response is not. When we uncover sin, we can resign ourselves to it, or we can hate it and cast ourselves on the unfathomable mercy and unending power of God. In other words, we have a choice. Either we can "fall into the hands of the living God" (10:31) and be consumed by his holy judgment, or we can willingly place ourselves into the hands of the living God, sinners that we are, and let the fire of his love burn away our sin and selfishness, layer by layer. Which will you choose?

"Lord, to whom can we go? You have the words of eternal life. We have come to believe and know that you are the Holy One of God" (John 6:68-69).

Hebrews 10:32-39

[32] But recall those earlier days when, after you had been enlightened, you endured a hard struggle with sufferings, [33]sometimes being publicly exposed to abuse and persecution, and sometimes being partners with those so treated. [34]For you had compassion for those who were in prison, and you cheerfully accepted the plundering of your possessions, knowing that you yourselves possessed something better and more lasting. [35]Do not, therefore, abandon that confidence of yours; it brings a great reward. [36]For you need endurance, so that when you have done the will of God, you may receive what was promised.
[37] For yet "in a very little while,
the one who is coming will come and will not delay;
[38] but my righteous one will live by faith.
My soul takes no pleasure in anyone who shrinks back."
[39]But we are not among those who shrink back and so are lost, but among those who have faith and so are saved.

My righteous one will live by faith. —Hebrews 10:38

I t was not easy being a Christian in the first century. Early believers suffered insults and sometimes even violence from neighbors
and government leaders. Many were imprisoned or had their prop-
erty seized. Yet, even in the face of such adversities, they "joyfully
accepted" being stripped of their belongings, knowing that they
"possessed something better and more lasting" (Hebrews 10:34).

Confidence in God's promises enabled the early Christians to endure
such hardship joyfully. By the time this letter was written, it had been
some years since those for whom it was intended had first come to
believe in Jesus. The regular joys and sufferings of life went on, and
their perseverance in hope continued to be tested. It was important
for these men and women to return constantly to the unshakable
knowledge that God is faithful to his promises.

In the twenty-first century, we face a similar challenge. In the face
of life's difficulties, we too are tempted to take our eyes away from God
and look elsewhere for solutions. The childless couple, the bankrupt
business owner, the laborer out of work—the list of those who are
tempted to lose hope in God is long, and eventually each of us finds
ourselves on it. Circumstances force us to examine whether we really
trust God's word. The world, the flesh, and the devil conspire to per-
suade us that God is distant and that, in the face of hardship, we are
left to our own resources.

Brothers and sisters, let us resist this false view of God! The Holy Spirit
wants to teach us that God is our loving Father. When we pray to him
in faith, we can experience his presence and know the reality of his love
in our lives. God wants to strengthen our faith, to be the rock on which
our lives are based. He allows trials so that we can learn how absolutely
reliable he is. By believing God's promises as we endure suffering, we learn
to love him perfectly, in preparation for eternal life with him.

"Father, I believe all you have spoken through Jesus. Help me to persevere in hope and to keep my gaze fixed on you. I trust you, Lord. Show me your will for my life today."

Hebrews 11:1-7

[1] Now faith is the assurance of things hoped for, the conviction of things not seen. [2]Indeed, by faith our ancestors received approval. [3]By faith we understand that the worlds were prepared by the word of God, so that what is seen was made from things that are not visible. [4] By faith Abel offered to God a more acceptable sacrifice than Cain's. Through this he received approval as righteous, God himself giving approval to his gifts; he died, but through his faith he still speaks. [5]By faith Enoch was taken so that he did not experience death; and "he was not found, because God had taken him." For it was attested before he was taken away that "he had pleased God." [6]And without faith it is impossible to please God, for whoever would approach him must believe that he exists and that he rewards those who seek him. [7]By faith Noah, warned by God about events as yet unseen, respected the warning and built an ark to save his household; by this he condemned the world and became an heir to the righteousness that is in accordance with faith.

Even the most hard-nosed atheist has firm convictions about many things he cannot see. We cannot see electricity, but when we flip the switch, we have faith that the lamp will turn on. If this doesn't happen, we check the plug, the fuse box, and the power lines to find out where the power has been interrupted.

We cannot see love, but we base our lives on the promise our spouse made at the altar. Every day we experience numerous proofs of his or her love. But people whose trust has been betrayed by abuse will find it difficult to believe that they are loved for their own sake. It may take a long time for them to stop looking for hidden motives, to relax and receive unconditional love without feeling compelled to pay everything back.

God's power is something like electricity. We can't see divine power, but we see its effects in the beauty of creation, in the orderly laws of nature, and in the miracles—great and small—that have occurred in our lives. God's love is even more like human love, full of surprises that go beyond all we expect and deserve. His power is often exercised on behalf of individuals, bringing physical healing, liberation from addiction to drugs, reconciliation between former enemies, and "Christ-incidences" that are difficult to explain except as personal gifts from an attentive parent.

Faith may sometimes feel like a leap into the unknown, but it really is a rational response to such manifestations of power and love. God has taken care of us in the past, so it is reasonable for me to trust him with today's needs. God's gift of faith is being able to trust with unshakable "assurance" and "conviction."

In this beautiful chapter dedicated to Old Testament heroes who put their faith into action, we see several facets of that faith. By faith, God's powerful word brought the universe into being—so let us never minimize the power of our own words to build up or tear down. By faith, Abel and Enoch discerned how to please God; they model for us the cost and the reward of personal sacrifice. By faith, those who have gone on ahead "still speak" to us, not only through our vivid memories but in the ongoing communion of saints, a treasure chest of resources for all our needs. By faith, Noah prepared with hope, trust, and energy for a future hidden from the eyes of the skeptics around him.

With them, let us "believe that [God] exists and that he rewards those who seek him" (Hebrews 11:6). Let's act on what we've already experienced to be true, and seek greater understanding and faith to push forward into the fullness of life God has for us in their company. The prayer of the sincere seeker is a guaranteed way to please God.

"Lord, I believe; help my unbelief."

Hebrews 11:8-19

8 By faith Abraham obeyed when he was called to set out for a place that he was to receive as an inheritance; and he set out, not knowing where he was going. 9By faith he stayed for a time in the land he had been promised, as in a foreign land, living in tents, as did Isaac and Jacob, who were heirs with him of the same promise. 10For he looked forward to the city that has foundations, whose architect and builder is God. 11By faith he received power of procreation, even though he was too old—and Sarah herself was barren—because he considered him faithful who had promised. 12Therefore from one person, and this one as good as dead, descendants were born, "as many as the stars of heaven and as the innumerable grains of sand by the seashore." 13 All of these died in faith without having received the promises, but from a distance they saw and greeted them. They confessed that

they were strangers and foreigners on the earth, [14]for people who speak in this way make it clear that they are seeking a homeland. [15]If they had been thinking of the land that they had left behind, they would have had opportunity to return. [16]But as it is, they desire a better country, that is, a heavenly one. Therefore God is not ashamed to be called their God; indeed, he has prepared a city for them.

[17] By faith Abraham, when put to the test, offered up Isaac. He who had received the promises was ready to offer up his only son, [18]of whom he had been told, "It is through Isaac that descendants shall be named for you." [19]He considered the fact that God is able even to raise someone from the dead—and figuratively speaking, he did receive him back.

F aith is one of the most intangible—yet one of the most important—aspects of our Christian life. Simply defined, it is a trust in the objective promises and realities of God. Abraham is probably one of the best examples of a life of faith. When God first called him, Abraham was an ordinary man, much like everyone around him. Yet as he responded to God, he became an extraordinary hero of faith who stands as a model, not only for us today, but for all believers of all times.

There must have been times when Abraham wondered whether he had misunderstood what God asked of him, or even if he had dreamed the whole thing up! Hearing God promise that he would be the father of many nations must have been wonderful, but that's when his troubles really began—a nomadic life, famine, war, and domestic strife. Yet God allowed each circumstance in order to build a disposition of trust and humble obedience in Abraham. Each new challenge gave him the opportunity to follow God's commands, even when doing so seemed to fly in the face of reason.

Without even telling Abraham the location, God told him to leave his home and set out for a foreign land (Genesis 12:10). And Abraham obeyed. He also had to reconcile God's promise to make him the father of nations with the fact that he and his wife were both aged and childless (15:1-6). Still, Abraham trusted and waited. Then, several years after the child was born, God asked Abraham to kill Isaac as a sacrificial offering (22:1-2). How could this be? Not only was Isaac his dearly loved son, he was also the one through whom God promised to bless all nations. But even then, Abraham proceeded in obedience to God's word, until an angel intervened. All these events took years to unfold. And it was in these years of waiting, trusting, and embracing each challenge as it came that Abraham was formed by God into a man of faith.

We too can become heroes of faith like Abraham. God only asks us to have an open heart and a willingness to follow wherever he leads. Let us yield ourselves to God, allowing him to form us into men and women of faith.

"Father, I don't want to run from the difficulties of life. Help me look to your promises and trust that you are forming me into your child. By your Spirit, help me to trust you more and more each day."

Hebrews 11:20-31

[20]By faith Isaac invoked blessings for the future on Jacob and Esau. [21]By faith Jacob, when dying, blessed each of the sons of Joseph, "bowing in worship over the top of his staff." [22]By faith Joseph, at the end of his life, made mention of the exodus of the Israelites and gave instructions about his burial.

²³ By faith Moses was hidden by his parents for three months after his birth, because they saw that the child was beautiful; and they were not afraid of the king's edict. ²⁴By faith Moses, when he was grown up, refused to be called a son of Pharaoh's daughter, ²⁵choosing rather to share ill-treatment with the people of God than to enjoy the fleeting pleasures of sin. ²⁶He considered abuse suffered for the Christ to be greater wealth than the treasures of Egypt, for he was looking ahead to the reward. ²⁷By faith he left Egypt, unafraid of the king's anger; for he persevered as though he saw him who is invisible. ²⁸By faith he kept the Passover and the sprinkling of blood, so that the destroyer of the firstborn would not touch the firstborn of Israel. ²⁹ By faith the people passed through the Red Sea as if it were dry land, but when the Egyptians attempted to do so they were drowned. ³⁰By faith the walls of Jericho fell after they had been encircled for seven days. ³¹By faith Rahab the prostitute did not perish with those who were disobedient, because she had received the spies in peace.

O ne of the sure signs that a child is beginning to mature is his ability to take a more long-term view of things. He's able to resist a late-afternoon snack to save room for a favorite dinner. Instead of spending his allowance on gum every week, he sets aside money for a LEGO set he really wants.

Becoming parents thrusts us forward into the future. Through nine months, we await the birth of a child and plan some of the ways our lives will change as a result. Even as we care for her immediate needs for food, warmth, and cleanliness, we open a bank account for her college education, pray for her future spouse, and consider how we will train her in etiquette and holiness.

The fathers in this passage definitely took the long view. The most important heritage Isaac, Jacob, and Joseph give their sons is not material things but their blessing—a blessing that has a tangible effect on the future. So forward-looking was Joseph that he gave careful instructions for how his remains were to be preserved for burial in the Promised Land, even though he had brought his whole family to settle with him in Egypt (Genesis 50:24-26). With forward-looking faith, Joseph trusted that his people's time in Egypt was only temporary.

Moses, too, was able to forego "the fleeting pleasures of sin" in order to be counted with God's chosen people, "shar[ing their] ill treatment" (Hebrews 11:25). Even though he only saw the Promised Land from a distant mountaintop, in faith he entered into his full inheritance. Rahab, the pagan harlot, also chose to turn her back on fleeting pleasures and find her new identity as one of the elect: ancestress of the Messiah.

What fleeting things bog us down today, diverting our gaze from the lasting prize? Some of us can be ensnared by pleasures we think we can't do without. Some are discontented with the hand God has dealt us today; we yield to the temptation to postpone fidelity and gratitude to an indefinite future when God finally gives us what we "deserve" and pine for. Some are too afraid to identify ourselves in the midst of a secular culture as believers in "him who is invisible" (Hebrews 11:27). Some feel intimidated by opposition from those who take themselves too seriously and make light of eternal values. Others feel weighted down like the Israelites at the edge of the Red Sea or at the gates of Jericho, seeing no human solution to their problems. But for all of us, the faith of our forefathers and foremothers can urge us on. God is on our side, and he is only waiting for us to cast our lot in with him.

"Father, lay your hands on our heads and give us your blessing. Help us preserve the rich heritage you have given us and carry it forward into a future full of hope."

Hebrews 11:32-40

[32] And what more should I say? For time would fail me to tell of Gideon, Barak, Samson, Jephthah, of David and Samuel and the prophets—[33]who through faith conquered kingdoms, administered justice, obtained promises, shut the mouths of lions, [34]quenched raging fire, escaped the edge of the sword, won strength out of weakness, became mighty in war, put foreign armies to flight. [35]Women received their dead by resurrection. Others were tortured, refusing to accept release, in order to obtain a better resurrection. [36]Others suffered mocking and flogging, and even chains and imprisonment. [37]They were stoned to death, they were sawn in two, they were killed by the sword; they went about in skins of sheep and goats, destitute, persecuted, tormented—[38]of whom the world was not worthy. They wandered in deserts and mountains, and in caves and holes in the ground.

[39] Yet all these, though they were commended for their faith, did not receive what was promised, [40]since God had provided something better so that they would not, apart from us, be made perfect.

Reading the exploits of the Old Testament saints is not the same as reading legendary tales of superhuman heroes. All those mentioned in Chapter 11 of Hebrews were ordinary people just like us. It was faith that made the difference and enabled them to witness the power of God despite their weaknesses.

The chapter begins with a definition of faith—"Faith is the assurance of things hoped for, the conviction of things not seen" (Hebrews 11:1)—and uses the word "faith" twenty-five times in the ensuing passage. Faith goes beyond intellectual assent to dogmas. It is the work of the Spirit in us that enables us to trust that what God has said is true and to base our lives and decisions on his word.

To have an active faith means that we put aside what our senses and emotions might tell us, and even what our experience may have shown us. We surrender our insistence on seeing the things of God on our own terms and take God's word as the basis of truth. Faith cannot come from ourselves.

Using examples from the time of the judges, kings, and prophets, the Letter to the Hebrews illustrates the blessings that result from trusting in God's promises. The exploits of Barak, Gideon, Jephthah, and Samson, and references to Daniel, David, Elijah, and Elisha testify to this legacy of faith and courage.

There are examples of the Maccabean family who were brutally tortured and killed rather than deny God (2 Maccabees 7); of Jeremiah, who—according to Jewish tradition—was stoned to death at the hands of the Jews in Egypt; and of Isaiah, who—also according to tradition—was sawed in half with a wooden saw. Their fortitude would be incomprehensible to one without faith.

We are called to bear witness along with these great believers. It is only *in Christ* that all of God's promises are brought to fruition. Along with those who have gone before us, we are numbered among the many sons and daughters being brought to glory in Christ Jesus. One day we will see this with our own eyes; for now, we walk by faith.

"Loving Father, I want to base my life on what your Son, Jesus, has done for us. Deliver me from the patterns of thinking that undermine your gift of faith. Lord, I believe. Help my unbelief!"

Hebrews 12:1-4

1 Therefore, since we are surrounded by so great a cloud of witnesses, let us also lay aside every weight and the sin that clings so closely, and let us run with perseverance the race that is set before us, 2looking to Jesus the pioneer and perfecter of our faith, who for the sake of the joy that was set before him endured the cross, disregarding its shame, and has taken his seat at the right hand of the throne of God.

3 Consider him who endured such hostility against himself from sinners, so that you may not grow weary or lose heart. 4In your struggle against sin you have not yet resisted to the point of shedding your blood.

The Christians to whom this letter was originally addressed had become a listless lot. Their community had once been zealous and had even suffered for the gospel (Hebrews 10:32). Now they had grown lax, wavering in their faith; some were no longer even meeting together (10:25). Perhaps these Christians were facing a renewed persecution, causing them to revert to their pre-Christian way of life. But whatever their situation, the author's answer to their problems remains the same as for believers of every era: Look to Jesus Christ.

The writer encouraged these Hebrew Christians with the example of holy people like Abraham, Isaac, and Jacob, who had overcome difficulties through faith (see Hebrews 11). In the author's imagery, these witnesses surround us as a great cloud, like a crowd in a stadium, urging us on like athletes in a spiritual race (12:1). Yet these Christians needed more than holy witnesses; they had to put their faith in Jesus, "the pioneer and perfecter of our faith" (12:2).

The Letter to the Hebrews makes one thing clear: Jesus is superior to everything in creation. He is greater than the angels (Hebrews 1:4), and Moses (3:3); he far surpasses the high priests (7:26-27), and his sacrifice makes theirs obsolete (9:13-14). This is because he has completely overthrown the power of the devil and death (2:14), has rightfully ascended to heaven, and "has taken his seat at the right hand of the throne of God" (12:2). We can place full confidence in Christ our mediator (4:14-16).

If we consider Jesus daily in prayer and Scripture, we will experience his power over our sinful, godless ways. His lordship will increase as we "lay aside . . . the sin that clings so closely" (Hebrews 12:1).

The Lord knows all his followers and the opposition they face, whether it arises from other people or from the interior struggle against sin. His message to us is not just to try harder to be blithely optimistic; rather, we must daily consider him "who for the sake of the joy that was set before him endured the cross" (Hebrews 12:2). His joy is the same as the joy that is set before us: everlasting life with God. His cross has already conquered our every sin. As we draw close to Jesus, we will find the desire and strength to serve him wholeheartedly.

"Loving Father, I ask you today to send me the Spirit of your Son, Jesus, that I might know him and serve him above all other things in my life."

Hebrews 12:4-13

[4]In your struggle against sin you have not yet resisted to the point of shedding your blood. [5]And you have forgotten the exhortation that addresses you as children—

"My child, do not regard lightly the discipline of the Lord,
or lose heart when you are punished by him;
6 for the Lord disciplines those whom he loves,
and chastises every child whom he accepts."
[7]Endure trials for the sake of discipline. God is treating you as children; for what child is there whom a parent does not discipline? [8]If you do not have that discipline in which all children share, then you are illegitimate and not his children. [9]Moreover, we had human parents to discipline us, and we respected them. Should we not be even more willing to be subject to the Father of spirits and live? [10]For they disciplined us for a short time as seemed best to them, but he disciplines us for our good, in order that we may share his holiness. [11]Now, discipline always seems painful rather than pleasant at the time, but later it yields the peaceful fruit of righteousness to those who have been trained by it.
12 Therefore lift your drooping hands and strengthen your weak knees, [13]and make straight paths for your feet, so that what is lame may not be put out of joint, but rather be healed.

Who wants to talk about discipline? Who especially wants to talk about God as a disciplinarian? Yet this is a necessary part of who God is and the role he plays as our heavenly Father. We can so easily look at God as a kindly old fellow who just wants us to be comfortable—more like a pleasant uncle than a father. But while God wants to comfort us in our difficulties, he is also interested in our personal growth and development, just like any good earthly father. For this reason, God will correct our faults and discipline us so that we can learn good habits and bear fruit in this world.

Oftentimes, God uses the natural consequences of our sins to correct us. St. Paul speaks of this process as reaping what we sow (Galatians 6:7-9). This discipline is for our own good. Tasting the bitter fruit of our misguided actions can help us see where we have gone wrong. Seeing the damage our sins have caused can move us to turn back to God. And if we do return, God will show us that he is disciplining us in love, not in anger or rejection.

Of course, not all suffering is the result of our failure. Tragedy may befall those who are making every effort to do God's will. Enemies may rise up unprovoked and attack those who have done them no harm. Yet God, in his fatherly love, can use these kinds of suffering also. The pain of sickness or injustice can drive us to cast ourselves on his mercy in ways we hadn't before. Suffering can reveal to us areas of shallowness in our goals and activities, and help us to refocus on what is truly important. Our own hardships can help us grow in compassion for the suffering of others. In these ways and more, God's loving discipline may be at work, calling us to a deeper intimacy with him. Is God trying to teach, correct, or discipline you? Trust in his wisdom and love.

"Father, give me a discerning heart to see how you are present in my difficulties and how I can cooperate with you. Give me the grace to repent when I have sinned, and the strength to endure suffering patiently. Above all, let these situations teach me how to abide with you continually."

Hebrews 12:14-17

[14] Pursue peace with everyone, and the holiness without which no one will see the Lord. [15]See to it that no one fails to obtain the grace of God; that no root of bitterness springs up and causes trou-

ble, and through it many become defiled. [16]See to it that no one becomes like Esau, an immoral and godless person, who sold his birthright for a single meal. [17]You know that later, when he wanted to inherit the blessing, he was rejected, for he found no chance to repent, even though he sought the blessing with tears.

I used to envision holiness as akin to a fragile, germ-free environment: something easily contaminated by the slightest misstep. But over time I've come to learn that holiness is the heritage Jesus has won for us by his death and resurrection. It is hardy and infectious, transforming everything we do and drawing others to share in God's overflowing life.

Similarly, the author of Hebrews tells us, "pursue peace with everyone" (Hebrews 12:14). Peace isn't the lack of conflict, a fragile state that requires walking gingerly lest we shatter it. The peace of God is robust, tangible, and transforming. It, too, is our heritage as sons and daughters of God. But we have to take hold of it deliberately and zealously. We have to "*see to it* that no one fails to obtain the grace of God; that no root of bitterness springs up and causes trouble, and through it many become defiled" (12:15).

After a fight, children often withdraw, barring their doors against the "enemy." They rehearse the ways in which they have been wronged, and refuse to accept responsibility for their own contribution to the conflict. The "root of bitterness" affects everyone around them, hanging over the household until everything is resolved. Sometimes parents are able to broker only an uneasy truce, a promise to leave each other alone.

This is reminiscent of Jacob and Esau, who wasted two decades of suspicion, separation, and hostility before being reconciled (Genesis 25:29–33:17). How much better when each combatant bravely admits his or her own contribution to the conflict, forgives the other from the heart, and sets out with the other to make things better!

Joined to the Son in baptism, everything God has given his beloved Son belongs to us as well. We don't have to bargain for it. Because his holiness is ours, we have eyes of faith to see the Lord at work in our lives and in his world. Through his gift of peace, we can seek and extend forgiveness every time we chip or fracture our relationship with one another. Because we are also called to share his cross, no suffering can isolate us from his love.

Let's pull out that root of bitterness that threatens our peace. Let's keep disagreements between ourselves and not gossip about them to others. Let's not open the door to memories of others' past wrongdoings, or uncharitable interpretations of their actions. Let's believe that they too are striving to please God and have our best interests at heart.

"Father, we thank you that 'in Christ we have also obtained an inheritance, having been destined according to the purpose of him who accomplishes all things according to his counsel and will, so that we . . . might live for the praise of his glory' (Ephesians 1:11-12)."

Hebrews 12:18-24

[18] You have not come to something that can be touched, a blazing fire, and darkness, and gloom, and a tempest, [19]and the sound of a trumpet, and a voice whose words made the hearers beg that not another word be spoken to them. [20] (For they could not endure the order that was given, "If even an animal touches the mountain, it shall be stoned to death." [21]Indeed, so terrifying was the sight that Moses said, "I tremble with fear.") [22]But you have come to Mount

Zion and to the city of the living God, the heavenly Jerusalem, and to innumerable angels in festal gathering, [23]and to the assembly of the firstborn who are enrolled in heaven, and to God the judge of all, and to the spirits of the righteous made perfect, [24]and to Jesus, the mediator of a new covenant, and to the sprinkled blood that speaks a better word than the blood of Abel.

With a clarity of vision that burned through the veil of the mundane, the author of Hebrews encouraged his readers with a glimpse of the hidden reality of worship. Whenever we pray—and especially when we celebrate the Eucharist—we come to "Mount Zion and to the city of the living God, . . . to innumerable angels, . . . to the assembly of the firstborn, . . . to Jesus, . . . and to the sprinkled blood" that he shed out of his love for us (Hebrews 12: 22-24). This is worship at its highest. In the presence of such glory, how can our hearts not be transformed?

The essence of Christian worship is communicating with our Father, opening our hearts to the Holy Spirit and receiving divine life through Jesus' body and blood. We are supremely blessed that—because of God's faithfulness to his promises—this always happens in our eucharistic celebration.

How do we receive this blessing? By faith, which is "the conviction of things not seen" (Hebrews 11:1). Such a perspective is both encouraging and daunting. How wonderful to believe that we are surrounded by angels at the Lord's table! How amazing that we can enter into the presence of God when we pray! And yet, who has not struggled at different times with feelings of emptiness or lack of fulfillment in prayer?

The answer lies not in a keener imagination or a sharper intellect. All we need is a continued openness to the transforming work of God.

He is present in our midst whenever we gather in his name, and he can transform even our most feeble efforts into a sacrifice of praise that truly touches our hearts. Bishop Faustus of Riez (*c.* 408–490) likened such an exchange to the way Jesus changed water into wine at the wedding in Cana:

> By Christ's action in Galilee, then, wine is made; that is, the law withdraws and grace takes its place; the shadows fade and truth becomes present; fleshly realities are coupled with spiritual, and the old covenant with its outward discipline is transformed into the new. For, as the Apostle says: the old order has passed away; now all is new! The water in the jars is not less than it was before, but now begins to be what it had not been. . . . When the wine fails, the new wine is served; the wine of the old covenant was good, but the wine of the new is better . . . the new covenant, which belongs to us, has the savor of life and is filled with grace.

"O God, open our hearts to your transforming power. Bless us with belief in the unseen so that we may receive the divine life that you offer us through Jesus in the Eucharist."

Hebrews 12:25-29

[25] See that you do not refuse the one who is speaking; for if they did not escape when they refused the one who warned them on earth, how much less will we escape if we reject the one who warns from heaven! [26]At that time his voice shook the earth; but now he

has promised, "Yet once more I will shake not only the earth but also the heaven." [27]This phrase, "Yet once more," indicates the removal of what is shaken—that is, created things—so that what cannot be shaken may remain. [28]Therefore, since we are receiving a kingdom that cannot be shaken, let us give thanks, by which we offer to God an acceptable worship with reverence and awe; [29]for indeed our God is a consuming fire.

See that you do not refuse the one who is speaking. —Hebrews 12:25

Have you ever experienced a calm, attentive discussion around the family dinner table? Or have you felt that nobody was really listening to what anyone else had to say? Some are too busy talking to listen. Some can't possibly wait their turn, afraid that their idea will be lost. Some make fun of another's manner of speaking. Some try to drown out what they fear may be a negative report about themselves. Sometimes a child will even put his fingers in his ears to block the one who is speaking.

Communication is the bond that holds human beings together. When we fail to listen to other people, we fail to connect with them on a personal level. We also miss out on what they have to say to us.

When we fail to listen to the people around us, we also run the risk of missing what God has to say to us. Of course, he sometimes speaks to us through Scripture or in the silent moments we spend alone in prayer; but his words also come out of other people's mouths. We only need to recognize them.

The voice of God is earthshaking. It loosens the hold of transitory things and invites us to base our lives firmly on the bedrock of the unchanging. It rocks old certainties to reveal unfathomable love. It invites us into the adventure of faith, where the path is not predetermined—only the destination and the unflappable guide for the journey.

When God's voice thundered from Mount Sinai, the Israelites were tempted to two extremes. If they ventured too close to the holy mountain, they would be consumed. If they stayed too far away, they would miss God's essential directions about how to live. The same temptations face us today. We may usurp the place that belongs to God, trying to determine by ourselves what is good and evil. Or we may keep God at arm's length, protesting that we are unworthy of grace and so failing to embrace the gifts God has entrusted to us.

"Our God is a consuming fire" (Hebrews 12:29). Our destiny is immolation. We can either be consumed by our own selfishness and the natural consequences of our own sins, or we can bring all we are to the fire and invite God to receive and purify us until nothing but his unshakable love is left.

"Father, many people and things can disappoint me and shake my faith. Help me to see that in you I am receiving 'a kingdom that cannot be shaken.' Help me to hear your voice and offer you 'acceptable worship with reverence and awe' (Hebrews 12:28)."

Hebrews 13:1-9

[1] Let mutual love continue. [2]Do not neglect to show hospitality to strangers, for by doing that some have entertained angels without knowing it. [3]Remember those who are in prison, as though you were in prison with them; those who are being tortured, as though you yourselves were being tortured. [4]Let marriage be held in honor by all, and let the marriage bed be kept undefiled; for

God will judge fornicators and adulterers. [5]Keep your lives free from the love of money, and be content with what you have; for he has said, "I will never leave you or forsake you." [6]So we can say with confidence,

"The Lord is my helper;

I will not be afraid.

What can anyone do to me?"

[7] Remember your leaders, those who spoke the word of God to you; consider the outcome of their way of life, and imitate their faith. [8]Jesus Christ is the same yesterday and today and forever. [9]Do not be carried away by all kinds of strange teachings; for it is well for the heart to be strengthened by grace, not by regulations about food, which have not benefited those who observe them.

Let mutual love continue. —*Hebrews 13:1*

What is the essence of our faith? Christianity is certainly more than a set of beliefs. First and foremost, it's a relationship— a communion of intimate love and friendship with God and with our neighbors. These two loves are inseparable. The more we experience God's love and love him in return, the more we will show our neighbor the mercy and kindness God has shown us.

Explaining how incredible this kind of love is, the author of the Letter to the Hebrews emphasizes its likeness to a family. He encourages us to treat one another with the kind of affection and loyalty that we would naturally give to our brothers and sisters. After all, through baptism we are all adopted sons and daughters of God, so recognizing our spiritual kinship with each other—even with those who are different from us—can help us to treat one another with great dignity and honor.

We naturally like to be around people who treat us well and benefit us in some way. But Christian love goes further. It reaches out to those who are difficult to love, who can be unkind, or who don't express their gratefulness. We can express this Christian fellowship and love in everyday acts of kindness, such as visiting the homebound, the lonely, and the sick. We can reach out to the homeless, the imprisoned, and the marginalized. It sounds idealistic, but such a love really is attainable. Why? Because "God's love has been poured into our hearts through the Holy Spirit" (Romans 5:5). It's that simple.

St. Augustine once wrote:

> Beg God for the gift to love one another. Love all people, even your enemies, not because they are your brothers and sisters. Love them in order that you may be at all times on fire with love, whether toward those who have become your brothers and sisters or toward your enemies, so that, by being beloved, they may become your brothers and sisters.

In the end, we will be judged not on the scope of our accomplishments, but on how well we have loved. Let us, then, beg God for the gift to love one another.

"Lord Jesus, your love surpasses all else. Fill my heart with compassion and mercy so that I may love my neighbor as you have loved me."

Hebrews 13:10-15

¹⁰We have an altar from which those who officiate in the tent have no right to eat. ¹¹For the bodies of those animals whose blood is brought into the sanctuary by the high priest as a sacrifice for sin are burned outside the camp. ¹²Therefore Jesus also suffered outside the city gate in order to sanctify the people by his own blood. ¹³Let us then go to him outside the camp and bear the abuse he endured. ¹⁴For here we have no lasting city, but we are looking for the city that is to come. ¹⁵Through him, then, let us continually offer a sacrifice of praise to God, that is, the fruit of lips that confess his name.

These verses recapitulate many of the recurring themes of Hebrews. We are sanctified by the blood of Christ. Because he was rejected and suffered for us, we who have been joined to him in baptism cannot expect a life of ease. Rather, we are invited to "go to him outside the camp and bear the abuse he endured" (Hebrews 13:13), to identify with the outcasts he came to redeem. Finally, "here we have no lasting city, but we are looking for the city that is to come" (13:14), the kingdom founded on God's unshakable fidelity and overwhelming mercy.

This unshakable kingdom is not a remote pie-in-the-sky hope but a present reality. In Verse 15, the writer indicates the doorway through which we can enter into that kingdom and abide there: praise. "Through him, then, let us continually offer a sacrifice of praise to God."

When unanticipated circumstances spoil our plans, what kind of words escape our mouths? Are they words of praise, placing ourselves and the new situation squarely in God's hands? Or are they the ugly hiss of griping and complaining?

Is it realistic or even possible to welcome every turn of events with praise? The writer gives us another key in his opening phrase, "through him." Praise does not spring naturally to our lips; it is the fruit of the indwelling Holy Spirit, who is always seeking to glorify the Father and advance his kingdom. Nor is praise usually spontaneous and effortless; the writer calls it "a sacrifice of praise." It often means setting aside what we had planned and stepping out of our comfort zone, trying to see things from God's perspective—or at least to discern our role in moving the situation closer to the reality of his kingdom.

Praise is "the fruit of lips that confess his name" (Hebrews 13:15). How often, and in what ways, does the name of God cross our lips? What is crucial here is not so much preaching about God as joining ourselves to him. A wise bishop once reminded a mother to spend much more time talking to God about her wayward children than talking to her children about God. Catholics of an earlier generation wrote "JMJ" (Jesus, Mary, Joseph) at the top of their school papers and frequently whispered the name of Jesus, or whatever form of address evoked worship at that moment: "Father," "Beloved Friend," "Suffering Savior." May we all evoke God so frequently!

"Jesus, you deserve all praise and glory! Let me pass my hours and days thanking you for the salvation you won for me on the cross, and for the kingdom you are building on the praises of your people."

Hebrews 13:16-21

[16] Do not neglect to do good and to share what you have, for such sacrifices are pleasing to God.

[17] Obey your leaders and submit to them, for they are keeping

watch over your souls and will give an account. Let them do this with joy and not with sighing—for that would be harmful to you. [18] Pray for us; we are sure that we have a clear conscience, desiring to act honorably in all things. [19]I urge you all the more to do this, so that I may be restored to you very soon.

[20] Now may the God of peace, who brought back from the dead our Lord Jesus, the great shepherd of the sheep, by the blood of the eternal covenant, [21]make you complete in everything good so that you may do his will, working among us that which is pleasing in his sight, through Jesus Christ, to whom be the glory forever and ever. Amen.

Thank you, Father, for setting a great shepherd over us, Jesus Christ, whom you chose from before the creation of the world. Jesus, the good shepherd (John 10:11), looks after us and tends to our needs. He is the one destined to go before us, making a path to you, Father, and opening the gates to heaven so we can be with you. Our shepherd reveals your love to us, and exhorts us, saying: "If you hear his voice, do not harden your hearts" (Hebrews 3:15). He is always calling to us: "Keep your hearts open and ready."

Thank you, Father, for equipping us with every good thing so that we can do your will. In Jesus, all your words in Scripture take on their ultimate meaning and give us hope for the eternal life to which you have called us. Your words hold the same power today as they did when they were first written down; through your word, you speak to our hearts, transforming us into your very image

Oh Lord, thank you for your provisions, which give life to our souls and joy to our hearts. You make us strong when we are weak, and hopeful in times of darkness. Help us keep our eyes on Jesus, our shepherd, so that we can remain faithful until you come again in glory.

Loving Father, thank you for giving up your Son, Jesus, our good shepherd, whose atoning blood has opened a way for us to know your love. We praise you and surrender our lives to you. We want to be living sacrifices, giving constant praise to your name. May every thought, action, word, and deed proclaim Jesus Christ our Lord. When we care for our families, may it be with the love and wisdom you have given us, thus allowing the world a glimpse of who you are. When we care for others, may we have the same mercy and compassion you have shown to us. As we cling to you in times of hardship, may we trust your faithfulness.

Most of all, dear Father, we pray that we will be witnesses to the power that your words in Scripture have for our lives today. Thank you for your love and provision. We open our hearts to your Holy Spirit. Pour into us the love and power of Jesus, that we may do his works.

Hebrews 13:22-25

22 I appeal to you, brothers and sisters, bear with my word of exhortation, for I have written to you briefly. 23I want you to know that our brother Timothy has been set free; and if he comes in time, he will be with me when I see you. 24Greet all your leaders and all the saints. Those from Italy send you greetings. 25Grace be with all of you.

What is on the author's heart and mind as he concludes this beautiful epistle? A final appeal to holiness through obedience, a bit of news, affectionate greetings, and the hope of seeing his readers again.

And what is on the reader's mind and heart? What new things have we learned from this study? What are we eager to share with others? What do we intend to carry forward into our daily lives in this outpost of the kingdom of God? What intercessions are we committed to presenting regularly before the throne of God?

"Greet all your leaders and all the saints. Those from Italy send you greetings" (Hebrews 13:24). These greetings were heartfelt even if they came from strangers who had never met in person. The thread that binds us together is grace (13:25), the grace we have all experienced and on which we depend.

So much of our conversation may seem trivial, but it is an essential part of building the kingdom, forging stronger bonds among the saints. How thoughtfully do we greet one another? When we say "How are you?" are we looking for a genuine answer or a quick platitude?

"Fine" isn't an adequate answer. We should want to know what each other has been thinking about, fretting over, or planning to change. Our own vision and heart can be greatly expanded as we tell each other where we have seen God working, and where we're still straining to discern his hand in challenging circumstances. We should all long to have eyes of faith that look beyond the surface and recognize each other as saints-in-the-making, people who bear God's very life, even if it is unpolished.

Perhaps even more challenging, we need to understand that we also are saints, members of God's chosen people, bound together in the body of Christ that transcends time and place. Our lives are interwoven with all the saints, including those who have completed their earthly journey and are available not only as shining examples but as faithful—and influential—intercessors.

It is claimed that any two persons on earth can trace a connection with no more than five human links between them. Our connection with every other Christian has only one degree: the living Christ. What richness lies in discovering the many facets of this kinship, the things we have in common and the unique gifts each of us brings to the table to benefit the whole body of Christ!

"Unnamed writer of the Letter to the Hebrews, we ask you to intercede for us, that we may discover the depths of divine mercy and our profound unity in the body of Christ."